One Good Thing:

The Psalms Part 1

30 Day Guide to Scripture Led Prayer

By Melissa Goepfrich

Melissa Goepfrich

www.melissagoepfrich.org

Contents

Introduction

What is the "one good thing?"

Spending quality time with the Lord is the most important part of every Christian's life. It is also the first thing that gets set to the side when life gets busy. In Luke chapter ten we are invited into the home of Mary and Martha to witness an encounter that should radically change our lives forever. Jesus drops in for a visit with a group of hungry young men. Martha went into hostess mode and began busying herself with cooking and working to welcome the men into her home. When she noticed that Mary was sitting at the feet of Jesus instead of helping her in the kitchen, she expressed her annoyance to Jesus. She wanted Him to tell Mary to get up and help with the work that Martha thought was necessary. Instead, this is what He responded:

"But the Lord answered and said to her, "Martha, Martha, you are worried and bothered about so many things; but only one thing is necessary, for Mary has chosen the good part, which shall not be taken away from her" (Luke 10:41-42).

The activities that Martha was spending time on were not sinful or wrong. There are a lot of activities that fill our schedules that are not necessarily bad. However, when we allow good things to overload our schedule we begin to be distracted and worried about these things, and we miss the one good thing that God says is necessary above all the others.

Your quiet time with your savior is the "one good thing." It involves both hearing from and talking to the one true God. The One who created you, loves you, died for you, and rose again to save you from your sin. We hear from God when we open His Word and read it. He is the author of Scripture and He wrote it for His children. If you want to know who God is and what He desires for your life, you must read the Scripture. We, in turn, talk to God through prayer. Without these two elements, you will not have a healthy relationship with the Lord. There are many devotionals out there designed to help you develop this relationship, but if you are not reading the Scripture and taking the time to pray, then you are simply adding another "feel good" moment into an already busy day. This book offers a practical guide to help you choose the good part – the one thing necessary – and get into the transformational Word of God.

Why this devotional series?

There is a riddle that asks the question, "How do you eat an elephant?" Deep fried with powdered sugar would be the most logical answer if you like to frequent the elephant ear booth at the local fair. One might even pose the question, "Is it even possible to eat an entire elephant?" Of course, we all know the answer to this common joke is "one bite at a time."

A similar question is often asked about reading the Bible. "How do you read the Bible?" It is a task seemingly impossible to most Christians today. The answer, if you have not guessed yet, is "one verse at a time." I know that reading Scripture can sound daunting. I know that you will not understand every sentence you read the first time you read it. God knows this too. It is ok! The more often you read and pray through Scripture, the better you will understand it over time. You will start to see how all the books of the Bible tie together. You will have plenty of "aha" moments if you just stick with it. Additionally, when you couple this daily interaction with God alongside regular church attendance and involvement in a solid Bible Study, you will begin to grow in your spiritual life by leaps and bounds.

Much like the task of reading Scripture, the prayer life of many Christians leaves something to be desired. Many Christian's "prayer life" consists of praying before meals, sometimes before bed, and listening while others pray at church. Maybe you throw up a quick prayer of "Lord, help me" in a frustrating situation. Possibly, you will reach the point in your prayer life where you keep a prayer list handy. You might take time every day (or at least once a week) to ask God to help the people on the list. These are all an important part of the Christian's prayer life, but they are missing a depth that you desperately need in your relationship with the Lord.

When I tell people how important it is to pray the Scripture, I am often met by blank stares. The truth is that Scripture is there for our teaching, reproof, correction, and training in righteousness (2 Tim 3:16). God's Word has everything in it that we need for life and godliness (1 Pet 1:3). Why then, would we not want to use God's word in conjunction with our prayer life? Scripture teaches us who God is and how we should address Him. Scripture contains the answers to the majority of the "why's" and "what's" that we so often ask in prayer.

Any relationship requires communication. This means listening to and talking to the one we are trying to build the relationship with. We listen to God through the reading of His Word, and we talk to God through prayer. Learning to pray through the Scripture is life changing.

The devotional book you are holding contains every aspect of a well-rounded quiet time with the Lord. Reading, meditation, instruction, prayer, Scripture memory, and basic practical application. This might seem like a long list to you, but these practices intertwine with each other so that you do many of them simultaneously. The amount of time you devote to each day is completely up to you. This book was designed to be rich enough for the seasoned Christian to be challenged to an even deeper one-on-one walk with God, but simple enough that the brand-new Christian can learn right away how to build and strengthen this new-found relationship. The more time you give to your meeting with the Lord, the more you will glean from His truth.

This is the first book in a series of devotional guides. Each book will consist of thirty days of devotions that will walk you through a specific section of Scripture. There will be 12 books in total that will cover the entire Bible from Genesis to Revelation.

I hope that you will be blessed. I am praying for you. I am praying that you will find understanding as you read. I am praying that your heart is open to accept God's truth as He has revealed it in Scripture. I am praying that you experience God in a way you never have before as you learn to pray alongside His Word. Most of all, I am praying that you would respond to God with a heart of obedience and submission to His will. I am praying that you are changed by this daily discipline.

User Guide

Before you begin this journey, take a moment to read through the following user guide. It will highlight each section that will appear every day and show you its purpose and function. Please, remember that this is only a guide to get you started in the habit of reading and praying through God's Word. Find a friend would can join you on this journey. Take the time to share with each other what God is teaching you.

Read and Meditate

I am often asked, "How do you hear from God?" Maybe you are desiring to hear a word from the Lord. Maybe you have felt like God speaks to others but is silent to you. Maybe you are discouraged and feel like you are not a good Christian because you do not "hear" from Him the way it seems other Christians do. I will tell you the same thing I tell everyone who asks me about this. Every time you open your Bible and read any part of Holy Scripture; you have just heard from God. He is the author of Scripture, and every single word is from Him. You might not understand it yet. You might not know how it applies to your life yet. You probably will not feel a huge wave of emotion most of the time, but you absolutely heard from Him. That is why the first part of every day of this devotional series will begin with reading God's Word so you can hear directly from Him.

Each day will include a few chapters of Scripture for you to read. Every other element of this devotional will come out of this daily section of reading. If you complete all twelve books, you will have read the entire Bible! Do not skip this part! Everything else after this step has the potential for human error. This step is the ONLY part that is 100% perfectly true, straight from God's mouth to your mind and heart. Always pray before you read, asking for understanding and teaching as you continue in your time with the Lord each day.

Learn

This section merits the least amount of attention. My words are not inspired, they are simply my best attempt to help you gain better understanding and maybe show you something you have not thought of yet in your overview of the passage. I bathe my writing in prayer, hoping that it is clear, accurate, and convicting. I have been a student of the Word for nearly forty years, yet I still have so much to learn. I hope that the little bit of knowledge and experience

God has allowed me will spill over to these pages and help draw you ever closer to your Savior.

Pray

You have already read the passage of the day, meditating on it for as long as you are able. You have read a short journaling entry from me about a small portion of the passage. Hopefully, you have already been in prayerful contemplation during the first steps. Now, it is time to allow the passage to guide your prayer time. Each day, I will share several specific verses that we will pray through together. I will share a brief prayer of my own and then leave space for you to write out your own prayer to the Lord. My prayer will be short and basic, taken from a more detailed prayer in my own devotion time. This should serve as a guide; a starting place for you to pray deeper and more specifically to your own situation. Do not stop with my verse choices! If you have more time in the day, take it even further and pray through other parts of the passage that God is using in your life.

Apply

Application is vital to the growing Christian's life. I will offer a couple of thoughts each day on action steps you might take in response to the day's passage. It might be something as simple as stepping outside to look at nature, offering thanksgiving to God for His creation. It might be something gut wrenching such as apologizing to someone you have offended. Do not take this step lightly. Make sure that you are prayerfully applying God's Word as You hear from Him. If God is showing you something completely different as you read and pray, please do not ignore it! Add to the action steps and commit to following God's Word – in *complete* obedience.

Memorize

We hide God's word in our hearts through Scripture memory. God tells us in Psalm 119:11 that the purpose of Scripture memory is so that we will not fall into sin. Jesus lived this out as an example to us when He was being tempted by the devil in the wilderness (Matt 4:1-11). Each time that Satan tempted Him, Jesus responded immediately with Scripture. If we are going to withstand temptation, we must memorize Scripture.

Each day, I will offer a small portion from the passage of the day for you to memorize. If another verse stands out more to you, then memorize that one instead. If you are overwhelmed with the thought of memorizing a new verse every day, then choose only one per week to work on. This book is simply a guide for you to take off and soar in your time with God. Adapt it to fit your life.

I understand that you may find it difficult to memorize. In the back of this book, I have included some practical ideas for methods of memory that might help you get started. God would not instruct us to do something that He has not equipped us for, and He clearly instructs us to hide His Word in our hearts. It is also known that those who regularly memorize Scripture have a much better memory overall. So, however you decide to go about it, make sure to give it a try!

Journal

I am a firm believer in journaling - and not just because I am a writer! God instructs us many times in Scripture to talk about His wonderful works and to tell the future generations all that He has done in our lives. I also know from experience how easy it is to get discouraged and forget everything God has done for me or taught to me over the years. In these times, when I am deeply struggling with my emotions and wondering where God is, I can return to my past journals. As I read through the pages of my past, I am quickly reminded of God's faithfulness. He speaks to me again through those same passages of Scripture and tells me to remember His wonderful works. He tells the deepest part of my heart and mind that He has never let me go, and He is not about to drop me now - hold on, you can get through this. I will leave space at the end of each day for you to record your own thoughts, prayers, and questions for future study. I would also recommend that you purchase a separate journal to use in conjunction with this devotional guide.

Day 1 – There is Safety in Godliness

Read and Meditate:

Psalm 1:1 – 4:8

Learn:

There is a common trend that runs through all of Scripture and all of time. Mankind cannot seem to faithfully serve and honor the God who created them. As a group, and individually, we have failed Him miserably, beginning with Adam and Eve in the garden. It was so bad at one point that God expressed sorrow that He ever created man, and He sent a flood to destroy all mankind (Gen 6:6). Thankfully, there was one righteous man, otherwise you would not be reading this because none of us would be here today.

My husband always says, "you cannot expect an unsaved person to act like they are saved." A born-again believer, on the other hand, should live differently than the unsaved world. The life of a Christian should line up with God's Word. He has given us the Holy Scripture to correct us and to teach us how we are to live this Christian life. That is why it is vital that we are reading and studying His Word. We must be sitting under sound teaching in a Bible preaching church. When we are consistently and properly immersing ourselves in the Bible, we will learn what our life should look like. Then, it is our responsibility to make the necessary changes in order to live in obedience to God.

Today's passage is filled with truth as the Psalmist asks questions of the Lord and of mankind. He wonders about the faithless living of men as they constantly seek after worthless things. He talks a great deal about the hope and joy that comes from seeking godliness over worldliness. The results are evident when the Psalmist declares, *"O Lord, make me to dwell in safety"* (Ps 4:8). There certainly is safety in living a life of obedience and godliness. Not a safety from physical harm, but the safety of knowing we are right in the center of God's will.

How often do you take stock of your life? Are you honoring the Lord with your life, or are you blending in with the world? Today's passage is filled with rich verses that make us take a hard look at how we respond to God. As you follow my lead in praying through a part of this passage, ask the Father to shine a light in your heart and point out all the ways that you need to turn from the lies of worldliness and turn to the safety of godliness.

Pray:

Psalm 4:1 – Answer me when I call, O God of my righteousness! You have relieved me in my distress; be gracious to me and hear my prayer.

My Prayer: God, You ARE my righteousness. I am nothing without you. I have nothing righteous in me besides you. Thank you for your gift of salvation. I do not deserve an audience with you, but I am asking, Lord, that You hear my prayers and answer my call to you today.

Your Prayer:

Psalm 4:2-3 – O sons of men, how long will my honor become a reproach? How long will you love what is worthless and aim at deception? Selah. But know that the Lord has set apart the godly man for Himself; the Lord hears when I call to Him.

My Prayer: Lord God, I bow in repentance at how ugly my heart is. Forgive me, Lord, for chasing after worthless things. God, I come to you broken, and humbly ask that you help me stay away from the sins that so easily trap me. Thank you for always being here when I come to meet with you.

Your Prayer:

Psalm 4:8 –In peace I will both lie down and sleep, for You alone, O Lord, make me to dwell in safety.

My Prayer: Thank You, God, for being my safe place. Thank You that I can always come to You and that You are always good. When I come to You and depend on You, You give me peace and joy even in the midst of trouble. Thank You for sustaining me and blessing me with Your peace.

Your Prayer:

Apply:

1. Identify one area of your life that reflects more of the current culture than it does the Bible.

2. Confess this area of your life to the Lord as sin and commit to being obedient to God's will instead of following the culture around you.

3. Make a list of ideas for changes that you might need to make in order to eliminate this sin from your life.

Memorize:

Psalm 1:1a – How blessed is the man who does not walk in the counsel of the wicked.

Journal Additional Prayers and Thoughts

Day 2 – Sin Hurts

Read and Meditate:

Psalm 5:1 – 7:17

Learn:

Raising children is not for the faint of heart. Sibling rivalry is a real thing and very often it can get out of hand. I often think about the fact that as believers, we are God's children and how sad it makes him when we fight. We taught a phrase to our children when they were young and in the throes of sibling rivalry. It is only two words, but it proved to pack a powerful punch in raising godly children. "Sin hurts." We would explain to them that when they sin, there were consequences. These consequences might be hurt feelings right now, or they could be a damaged relationship for the rest of their life.

Sin hurts the sinner and it also hurts others who are near the sinner. It hurts the sinner when they are disciplined, but much more than that, the sin hurts their heart and spirit. Until they repent and seek forgiveness, that sin festers in their heart, building callouses and walls. It also hurts the people around them. How it hurts depends on what the sin is, but it can be physical, emotional, mental, or even spiritual. We also made sure they knew that sin hurts God. The gospel of Jesus Christ was shared in our home with our children often. They knew from a young age that sin is the reason that Jesus had to die on the cross. This was just one way that we were able to help their little hearts grasp the reality of sin, discipline, and grace. Sin hurts.

In today's passage, David shares just how much sin hurts. He pours his heart out, sharing how he spent every night drowning his pillow with tears of sorrow. If ever there was someone in the Bible who suffered from depression, it was David. This time, it was the result of other people committing sins against God that had a direct impact on his own life; and it hurt. He begins Psalm 6 by recognizing his own sinful tendencies. David asked for graciousness and for God to hold back His wrath from him. He cries to the Lord, sharing how he is hurt by the action of his enemies. He even goes so far as to say that all his enemies will be ashamed when they are forced to turn away and he is honored by God. He trusted God's promises to protect, comfort, and heal his hurt.

How do you deal with the hurt of sin? Hopefully, you take it to the Lord and are honest about your hurt as well as the hurt you have caused others. Remember that sin hurts as you pray through a portion of today's passage.

Pray:

Psalm 6:1-3 – O Lord, do not rebuke me in Your anger, nor chasten me in Your wrath. Be gracious to me, O Lord, for I am pining away; Heal me, O Lord, for my bones are dismayed. And my soul is greatly dismayed; but You, O Lord – how long?

My Prayer: Lord God, my heart is overwhelmed right now. The trials and attacks seem never-ending. I know I am a sinner, and I know I deserve Your wrath. Thank You for saving me and not pouring Your wrath out on me. God, You alone can bring the healing to my body and spirit.

Your Prayer:

Psalm 6:6-7 – I am weary with my sighing; every night I make my bed swim, I dissolve my couch with my tears. My eye has wasted away with grief; it has become old because of all my adversaries.

My Prayer: Lord, I don't want to be discouraged any more. I am tired of the onslaught of emotions that drown me. I need You, God. I need You to remind me of truth. Remind me who You are. Thank You for my weakness and for my tears. Show me how to use this grief to glorify and honor You, Lord.

Your Prayer:

Psalm 6:9-10 –The Lord has heard my supplication, the Lord receives my prayer. All my enemies will be ashamed and greatly dismayed; They shall turn back, they will suddenly be ashamed.

My Prayer: Oh, God, there are so many who have hurt me in their iniquity. I ask You to reveal to me anyone who I have hurt by my own sins. Forgive me for the hurts that my sin has caused to others. Keep me sensitive to Your Spirit's conviction.

Your Prayer:

Apply:

1. Make a list of people whose sins are dragging you down or hurting you.

2. Now make a list of anyone you have hurt by your own sinful behavior.

3. Pray over these lists name by name.

4. If restoration is possible, take time to talk with these people.

5. If boundaries are needed, allow the Lord to guide you to deal with these relationships for His glory.

Memorize:

Psalm 6:9 – The Lord has heard my supplication, the Lord receives my prayer.

Journal Additional Prayers and Thoughts

.

Day 3 – Perspective Matters

Read and Meditate:

Psalm 8:1 – 10:18

Learn:

It is easy for us to get caught up in our own life and lose sight of the bigger picture. When we are in the middle of daily life, everything seems to revolve around us because we are there for all of it. Naturally, we look at the details of life, both good and bad, and allow those details to elate us or overwhelm us. When things are going very well for us, we feel good about life. When life gets tough, we start shutting down. Often, we allow this self-focus to hinder our relationships with others and even with God.

Today's passage helps to bring our life back into right perspective. Whenever I read Psalm 8 specifically, I become completely overwhelmed. Life is so much bigger than just me. In fact, when I put my eyes on how huge my God is, and I look around at the vast expanse of just the parts of the universe that I can see with the naked eye, I realize that I am nothing. My life is like a speck on a piece of dust floating around on a pin head. My lifespan is just a blip on the radar of eternity. I am nothing. I know my sin, I know my weaknesses, I know my place before God and I know that it is only by the grace of God and the blood of Jesus that I have any hope at all in this life and the next.

Then I read Psalm 8. Without the proper perspective of who God is, it would be easy to read this passage to feed my own ego. Instead, like the Psalmist, I fall to my knees unworthy. I recognize that life is bigger than me. Only God is worthy, and yet God has chosen to crown me with glory and majesty! What?! That should shake you to the core. It should drive you and me to our knees in gratitude. It should cause us to pause, look at our life, and make sure we are living it worthy of this high calling that God has given us.

What does your world revolve around? Your career? Your children? Your status and success in life? The pleasures of life you have grown to love? Do you recognize how big your God is? It is important to understand your place before God. Then when you wonder, as the Psalmist often did, why God seems so far away you will remember that He values you so much more than you value Him. He hears you; He strengthens you; He is there for you every minute of every day. Evaluate your perspective as you pray through today's passage.

Pray:

Psalm 8:1 – O Lord, our Lord, how majestic is Your name in all the earth, who have displayed Your splendor above the heavens!

My Prayer: God, Your name is great, and mighty, and worthy to be praised. Nothing in this world can compare to who You are and the power You hold. Thank You for being my strength. Thank You for choosing me. I was Your enemy, but You have saved me!

Your Prayer:

Psalm 8:3-5 – When I consider Your heavens, the work of Your fingers, the moon and the stars, which You have ordained; what is man that You take thought of him, and the son of man that You care for him? Yet You have made him a little lower than God, and You crown Him with glory and majesty!

My Prayer: I am unworthy Lord. I am nothing; a sinner fallen so far short of Your glory. I do not understand how

You - who created the vastness of the entire universe with just a WORD - would choose to glorify me, a worm. How could You crown me with glory and majesty when it is You and You alone who is worthy of such honor? Thank You for giving me value, purpose, and worth as I reflect Your glory, Lord.

Your Prayer:

Psalm 8:9 – O Lord, our Lord, how majestic is Your name in all the earth!

My Prayer: Your name is awesome, amazing, full of honor, glory, and majesty, worthy of all my praise! Every ounce of my worship belongs to You Lord. Forgive me when my worship shifts to things that do not deserve it. You are the only one who deserves my worship. Thank You for Your majesty!

Your Prayer:

Apply:

1. Go outside and look at the sky at different times of the day and night. Allow yourself to stare at it for a while, looking around as far as you can see. Notice the colors, the cloud formations, the vastness of it all. Try to count the stars on a clear night.
2. Journal about what you notice, giving God praise and honor for His creation.
3. Next time you are overwhelmed with your life, go back to your journal and remember that it is not about you.
4. Thank God for the beauty of His creation and for allowing you to be a part of it all.

Memorize:

Psalm 8:4-5 – What is man that You take thought of him, and the son of man that You care for him? Yet You have made him a little lower than God, and You crown him with glory and majesty!

Journal Additional Prayers and Thoughts

Day 4 – A Faithless Generation

Read and Meditate:

Psalm 11:1 – 13:6

Learn:

The number of Christians who are being deceived by our post-modern culture of "Christianity" is staggering. Standing on the truth of Scripture makes us "haters" in today's world. Since we want to be known as "lovers" instead of "haters," we cower from the truth so as not to hurt anyone's feelings. The world is going to stand against Christianity; that is nothing new. I expect the unbelieving world to live in sin and to push their views. What is disturbing is that so many Christians are being swayed into thinking that the views and ideals of the unbelieving world have any kind of place inside the church of the Living God! They do not!

We must be vigilant, as Christians, to learn the truth of Scripture so that we are not swayed by smooth-talking, cunning deceivers who are constantly creeping into our churches and into our homes. They show up on TV programs, radio shows, social media, and yes, even in our church meetings. What they have to say might sound good.

Their words match the type of "Christianity" that so many have conceived in their own minds. They focus on love, prosperity, and social justice. They cleverly avoid any talk about sin, judgement, and hell. They do not give the full picture of true Christianity as seen in God's Word. Today's passage tore me up a little as, once again, I poured out my heart to God over the evil that is rampaging – not just the world – but the church as well.

Pray with me! Ask God to search your heart and point out where you have been believing the lies of those with flattering lips and double hearts. Ask God for wisdom and discernment when you hear a message, read a book, or follow a popular teacher. Pray for your church and for all Christians around the world that we would return to truth and sound doctrine.

Pray:
Psalm 11:1a – In the Lord I take refuge;

My Prayer: Thank You, Lord, for being my refuge. You are my safe place, the One who holds me in His hand. The days are getting darker and darker and I need Your safety, Your comfort, and Your strength.

Your Prayer:

Psalm 12:1-4 – Help, Lord, for the godly man ceases to be, for the faithful disappear from among the sons of men. They speak falsehood to one another; with flattering lips and with a double heart they speak. May the Lord cut off all flattering lips, the tongue that speaks great things; who have said, "With our tongue we will prevail; our lips are our own; who is lord over us?"

My Prayer: Lord God, where have all the faithful gone? There are so many who profess Christ and yet live in the mindset of the world and not Your Word. Forgive us, Lord! Destroy those who are propagating lies. Remove them from our churches and from Christian homes. Exalt those who speak Your truth without shame. Lord, bring the masses to those preachers who are not afraid to tell Your truth boldly. Open the mouth of the ones who are afraid of being criticized. Stir us up, Lord!

Your Prayer:

Psalm 13:5-6 – But I have trusted in Your lovingkindness; My heart shall rejoice in Your salvation. I will sing to the Lord, because He has dealt bountifully with me.

My Prayer: I do trust You Lord, even when the waiting is hard. Your salvation and lovingkindness toward me are the only thing I need. You are enough for me, even when everything else is falling apart. Your salvation is permanent and secure. Your lovingkindness is beautiful and undeserved. Thank You, Lord, for Your bountiful mercies toward me. Remind me of every blessing every day. My praise goes to You and You alone.

Your Prayer:

Apply:

1. In what ways have you been unfaithful? Confess it to the Lord and ask His forgiveness.

2. What influences have you allowed into your life that talk "spiritual" but not biblical? Cut them out of your life today!

3. Are you waiting on the Lord for something? Write it out; every detail. Then, write down a list of all your possessions and all the loved ones in your life. (I bet you quit from fatigue before you finish the list!)

4. Now, turn on some worship music and sing to the Lord as you thank Him for these blessings and trust Him in your waiting.

Memorize:

Psalm 13:5-6 – But I have trusted in Your lovingkindness; My heart shall rejoice in Your salvation. I will sing to the Lord, because He has dealt bountifully with me.

Journal Additional Prayers and Thoughts

Day 5 – The Counsel of Fools

Read and Meditate:
Psalm 14:1 – 16:11

Learn:

What if I told you that you have full access to the absolute best counseling in the world? This counselor is not only experienced in every form of counseling, but He already knows every detail of your heart. He does not have to spend weeks collecting data in order to get a snapshot of your life with which to formulate an opinion on who you are and what you are going through. You do not need to worry about lying to Him or trying to not sound too troubled because He already knows the deepest thoughts of your heart. He has seen every move, every thought, every attitude in your heart from the day you were born. He knows exactly what you are dealing with and He knows exactly how to counsel you to get you through it. His advice can be followed explicitly without fear of making a wrong decision.

Every believer has the same access to God, who is the perfect counselor. Why then, are so many Christians getting their counsel from worldly sources? The world ignores God, and the Psalmist today calls them fools. The world does not have the answers for life; God does, and He has revealed them to us in His Word.

I am a huge fan of counseling. The Bible affirms that we need wise counsel in our lives on a regular basis. I have counseled hundreds of people throughout my life, and I have sought out counsel for myself on every level. Counseling is a necessity in the life of a Christian. It is good. The danger comes in when we seek out the wrong type of counsel. As a Christian, we should desire sound, biblical counsel. Any counsel that does not line up with God's Word is foolish.

So, how do you know if you are listening to foolish counsel or godly counsel? There are two methods that you can use. The first is to dig through the Scripture every time you receive counsel and see if what was said matches what God has said. This method can work, but if you are not familiar with God's Word you might quickly become confused.

The second method is the one that works the best and offers the most permanent solution. You must dedicate your life to reading, studying, and memorizing God's Word. You must spend time in God's Word and in prayer every single day. You might still have some confusion in the beginning, but only with this lifestyle shift of truly learning truth will you be equipped to recognize foolish counsel.

Pray:

Psalm 16:1-2 – Preserve me, O God, for I take refuge in You. I said to the Lord, "You are my Lord; I have no good besides You."

My Prayer: You ARE my God, and I am so grateful for You. I know that there is nothing good in my life that has not come from You. You are good, and You are the source of all good. I know that even when things are bad in my life, there is still good there. Thank You for the good. I pray that as You preserve me (keep me safe) that you preserve ALL of me. Keep my mind safe from the attacks of the enemy. Keep my heart safe from the world.

Your Prayer:

Psalm 16:7 – I will bless the Lord who has counseled me; Indeed, my mind instructs me in the night.

My Prayer: Your counsel is perfect every time, God. Forgive me when I ignore it. Thank You for Your gentle whisper to my mind. Thank You for Your Word that instructs me how I should live. I feel safe coming to You with every anxiety and hardship. You hold me when I am crying, and You rejoice with me when I am happy.

Your Prayer:

Psalm 16:8-9 – I have set the Lord continually before me; because He is at my right hand, I will not be shaken. Therefore my heart is glad and my glory rejoices; my flesh also will dwell securely.

My Prayer: I am secure in You and You alone. Only in You do I rejoice because every joy I have comes from You. Every day I need You present and visible to me. Thank You for never leaving.

Your Prayer:

Apply:

Where do you get your counsel from? Your friends, magazines, Facebook, authors, talk shows?

1. Make a list of the names of all the sources of advice or counsel that are in your life currently.
2. Take your list to your pastor, pastor's wife, or another trusted spiritual leader and ask them to go through it with you and help you get rid of anything that is foolish counsel.
3. Commit today to add more Bible and prayer into your daily life and to take your counsel only from biblical sources.

Memorize:

Psalm 16:8 – I have set the Lord continually before me; because He is at my right hand, I will not be shaken.

Journal Additional Prayers and Thoughts

Day 6 – Trust the Sovereignty of God

Read and Meditate:

Psalm 17:1 – 18:50

Learn:

There is no question that David knew, beyond a shadow of a doubt, that God would hear him when he called. Notice how many times throughout the Psalms he mentions crying out to God because He is worthy, and He hears. I have had many struggles throughout my lifetime that often led to bouts of depression. I am so thankful that God taught me at a very young age that He is with me and hears me every time I cry out to Him.

When I feel the heavy weight of discouragement trying to creep into my heart and weigh me down, I immediately increase the amount of time I spend in God's Word and in prayer. His truth keeps the right perspective in my mind. It is almost always my circumstances that begin a wave of discouragement, but it is when I view my problems as bigger than my God that the downward spiral to depression begins. I need to remember every day that God hears me and that He is infinitely greater than my circumstances.

Discouragement can still drag us down, even amid closely walking with the Lord. This often happens when we lose sight of the sovereignty of God. Sovereignty means that God can do what He wants, when He wants, how He wants, to whomever He wants, at any given time. It means that He is in complete control and that He always knows what He's doing and why He's doing it. We are not sovereign. We do not know the "what" and "why" of most circumstances.

Did you notice in this passage how many times the Psalmist mentions "You" in reference to God and what He is doing? He cries out to God, and then he recognizes that whatever happened was of God. He talks about the difference between his faithfulness versus the sinful patterns of the wicked, but the results and actions toward both the faithful and the wicked came from the hand of God. We can come to the Lord in complete honesty, total vulnerability, and absolute trust that He is going to do whatever His will is for our lives. Our job – and what trips me up from time to time – is to trust God's timing and His will.

Lord, help us to always trust You! When You bless us beyond our wildest dreams, help us to be grateful. When You allow trials and struggles that seem to drown us, help us thank You and lean on You to get us through the storm. Build in us a heart like David. Obedient. Faithful. Steadfast. Trusting.

Pray:

Psalm 17:1 – Hear a just cause, O Lord, give heed to my cry; give ear to my prayer, which is not from deceitful lips.

My Prayer: Lord, search my heart, and see that the prayers I bring are from the honesty of my heart. May I never try to trick You or deceive You. Who am I that I would ever be able to hide the truth from You? Lord, if my perspective is wrong, please change it. If my prayers are of just cause, I know that You will answer them because you are a just God. Thank You for hearing my prayers always.

Your Prayer:

Psalm 18:6 – In my distress I called upon the Lord, and cried to my God for help;

My Prayer: I am here, again, crying out to You from a place of sorrow and agony. I call to You, knowing full well that You listen; You hear me, and You will answer me. I trust Your answer, and I trust Your timing.

Your Prayer:

Psalm 18:19 – He brought me forth also into a broad place; He rescued me, because He delighted in me.

My Prayer: Thank You for setting my feet on solid ground every time I come to You in truth. I do not know why You delight in me but knowing that You do gives me confidence and grace. I know that You will once again deliver me from the distress that I am in. I know that You will always rescue me when I call, and for that I am extremely grateful!

Your Prayer:

Apply:

1. Read today's passage again and make a list of every time the Psalmist says "You" or "The Lord" referencing something God is doing. You can simply underline or circle each one in your Bible, or you can write out a list in your journal.

2. Now, make another list of all the circumstances that are currently a part of your life. This could include your job, church, home, people, trials, or blessings. Be detailed, and list as many as you can.

3. In front of every item on your list, write the words "God did," or "God allowed," or "God gave," etc. – whatever fits the circumstance that shows that it came from God.

4. Use this visual as you pray again, asking God to search your heart and reveal how much you truly trust Him. Talk to Him about that!

Memorize:

Psalm 18:1-2 – I love you, O Lord, My strength. The Lord is my rock and my fortress and my deliverer, My God, my rock, in whom I take refuge; My shield and the horn of my salvation, my stronghold.

Journal Additional Prayers and Thoughts

Day 7 – The Desirable Way of the Lord

Read and Meditate:

Psalm 19:1 – 21:13

Learn:

Think about the most valuable possession in your life; that one thing you desire more than anything in the whole world. Can you picture it? Do you already own it, or are you still waiting for it? If you are still waiting, what would you do to get it? If you already have it, how hard are you working to keep it or protect it?

In Psalm 19, God shows us what should be the most valuable possessions of one who loves the Lord. Loving and keeping the ways of the Lord are of so much greater value than my dearest possession and, yes, even greater than the most valuable people in my life! As believers, we should desire to follow God's ways, which means that we should do whatever it takes to learn His ways, to guard His truth in our life, and to live out what He has told us to do.

I love to make charts when I come across a passage of Scripture that has a list of some sort. Often, when I am in my daily quiet time, I will mark something that I want to look at for deeper study in the future. I encourage you to make that a part of your daily time with the Lord as well.

I want to share with you the chart I made from Psalm 19:7-9, and I encourage you to take some time later to study this passage. The chart reveals what God says is more desirable than gold (the most precious possession of that day), why it is to be desired, and how it works in our daily life. In Psalm 19:11 we are both warned by them as well as promised reward in keeping them. Perhaps the warning is against the natural consequences that come from ignoring these things. Praise God for His rewards to those who faithfully follow His ways!

What	Why	How
Law	Perfect	Restores the soul
Testimony	Sure	Simple made wise
Precepts	Right	Rejoices the heart
Commandment	Pure	Enlightens the eyes
Fear	Clean	Endures forever
Judgments	True	Righteous altogether

Pray:

Psalm 19:10-11 – They are more desirable than gold, yes, than much fine gold; sweeter also than honey and the drippings of the honeycomb. Moreover, by them Your servant is warned; in keeping them there is great reward.

My Prayer: Lord, put Your desires in my heart. I have opened it up to You to fill with Your ways and Your truths. Create an even deeper longing and desire to follow Your ways and draw ever close to You. Thank You for all the many blessings that You have rewarded me with. I look forward to the day that I get to be with You, my greatest reward of all, in person!

Your Prayer:

Psalm 19:14 – Let the words of my mouth and the meditation of my heart be acceptable in Your sight, O Lord, my rock and my Redeemer.

My Prayer: God, I pray that You would guard my tongue. Continue to change my heart so that my words and my thoughts will be pleasing to You.

Your Prayer:

Psalm 21:7 – For the king trusts in the Lord, and through the lovingkindness of the Most High he will not be shaken.

My Prayer: Lord, give me faith like David, that I would trust You so much that I would be unshakable. When storms arise and threaten to steal my joy, I pray that You would remind me of this verse and that I would take comfort in Your mercy toward me.

Your Prayer:

Apply:

1. Review the list from Psalm 19.
2. Is there a command that you are ignoring?
3. Do you question any of God's judgments?
4. Make a list and confess those to the Lord.

Memorize:

Psalm 19:14 – Let the words of my mouth and the meditation of my heart be acceptable in Your sight, O Lord, my rock and my Redeemer.

Journal Additional Prayers and Thoughts

Day 8 – The Struggles of Christ

Read and Meditate:

Psalm 22:1 – 24:10

Learn:

Do you ever feel like God has turned His back on you? Maybe you are going through one of the hardest trials of your life, and you are not hearing anything from the Lord. The truth is, there are times in our lives when God is just silent. What do we do? How do we live in the silence? Today's passage gives us a glimpse into the life of Jesus to answer these questions.

We do not often think about Jesus as having struggles. We tend to focus more on His deity than we do His humanity. Yes, He is 100% God, but He is also 100% man. It is one of the great, mysterious truths that we are not supposed to understand in our finite minds, but it is one we must acknowledge as we learn Scripture and apply it to our lives. We get several glimpses throughout Scripture into the prayer life of Christ. Psalm 22 is one of those passages as David writes the very words that Jesus later prays while hanging on the cross. Pay attention to how Jesus prayed regarding the cross. God was silent. His enemies were prevailing. His body was mutilated. He strength was gone. He was crying out for help and deliverance, and God was silent. He heard Him, yet He remained silent.

Jesus knows what it feels like to struggle and to feel all alone, yet He remained faithful and obedient to die on the cross because that was what His Father commanded Him to do. He suffered and died so that you and I could have life if we so choose it. He has given us a beautiful example to follow when we feel all alone in our sufferings. We cry out to the Lord continually. We do not quit. We obey Him in everything as we cry out for help. We trust Him completely – that if He does not deliver, He has a greater purpose. We still pray. We still obey. We still trust.

Pray:
Psalm 22:1-3 – My God, my God, why have You forsaken me? Far from my deliverance are the words of my groaning. O my God, I cry by day, but You do not answer; And by night, but I have no rest. Yet You are holy, O You who are enthroned upon the praises of Israel.

My Prayer: I confess that I often feel like You are not there, God. In my flesh I am weak, and I get lost in my emotions and the stressful circumstances of life. I often cry out to

You for deliverance, and You are silent. Lord, in my humanity, I struggle with that so much. Yet, I know that You are holy. I know that You are God, and I am not. I know that You see all, and if You are allowing it, then it is for Your good glory. Help me remember Your holiness when I am in these times.

Your Prayer:

Psalm 22:11 – Be not far from me, for trouble is near; for there is none to help.

My Prayer: God, my reality is that life gets hard. People are mean sometimes, and they like to cause a lot of trouble. Often, I feel like there is no one who can help in our current circumstances. Be my help, O Lord. Please be near me in very real ways and be my help. I cannot live this life on my own, and I need Your daily presence to get through. Thank You for being my God and for never leaving me.

Your Prayer:

Psalm 22:15a – My strength is dried up…

My Prayer: Lord God, I have nothing left in me. I am worn out, beaten down, and void of the strength needed to move forward. You are my strength! You know full well, as the Son of God hung on the cross, what it is like to be without strength. Thank You for reminding me that I am not alone, that you know how I feel, and You felt it infinitely greater than I. Be my strength and my deliverer in the shadows of this life. Thank You for Psalm 23 and the beautiful reminder that You are my Good Shepherd who is looking out for me. You do not want me to stay wounded, but You want to set me on solid ground and heal every part of me. I need You every day, Lord God.

Your Prayer:

Apply:

1. Are you lacking strength right now? Write out your struggles and compare them to the description of Christ on the cross in Psalm 22.

2. Knowing that He understands, write the words, "I will trust and obey" next to every single struggle you wrote down.

3. Keep crying out to the Lord as you trust and obey Him this week.

Memorize:

Psalm 22:24 – For He has not despised nor abhorred the affliction of the afflicted; Nor has He hidden His face from him; But when he cried to Him for help, He heard.

Journal Additional Prayers and Thoughts

Day 9 – Wait on the Lord

Read and Meditate:

Psalm 25:1 – 26:12

Learn:

  I despise waiting. I am not naturally a patient person. I am the absolute worst around birthdays and Christmas! I usually wait until the very last minute to buy a gift for someone in my family because I cannot hold on to it once I have it. The gift sometimes does not even make it into wrapping paper before I am excitedly handing it over to its recipient, sometimes days or even weeks before the big day. I am also nearly impossible to surprise. If I get even the slightest hint that there is something being planned for me, or a gift waiting for me, I am in all out CIA mode trying to get to the bottom of it and see what is awaiting me. Once I know something is coming, I am miserable because I still must wait for it.

  I am not any better when it comes to waiting on God. Whether it is waiting on Him to deliver me from a storm, waiting for something I think He has for me, or simply waiting for His return I am just antsy. I do not like to wait. It is really no wonder then that God has put me in some serious times of waiting throughout my life. He patiently teaches me how to wait, and how to enjoy the waiting. He graciously forgives me when I run ahead of Him and make a mess of things. I still do not like to wait, but I am learning how to wait.

Maybe you are in a season of waiting. It might be, as the Psalmist displays in today's passage, that you are waiting for deliverance from an enemy. You may have been praying for years for a family member to come back to the Lord. Possibly, you are facing a time of discouragement in your job or even in your church and you are waiting for it to turn around. Whatever the situation you are waiting on God for, the question arises; what does it look like to wait on God?

We wait in complete and utter trust in His sovereignty. We trust Him to know what to bring to our lives and when to bring it. We accept it when God makes it clear that we are waiting for the wrong things and we need to let it go. We serve Him in active obedience while we wait for what is next. We live – I mean really LIVE – while we are waiting; enjoying the journey that God has us on. What is not acceptable is falling into sin because we are tired of waiting. We must stand firm in our integrity even when we are overwhelmed with the circumstances we are in as we wait on the Lord.

Pray:

Psalm 25:4-5 - Make me know Your ways, O Lord; teach me Your paths. Lead me in Your truth and teach me, for You are the God of my salvation; for You I wait all the day.

My Prayer: Lord God, teach me to wait on You. I have seen Your faithfulness over and over in my life and I know that waiting on You is so much better than doing it myself. I want to walk in Your paths.

Your Prayer:

Psalm 25:16-18 – Turn to me and be gracious to me, for I am lonely and afflicted. The troubles of my heart are enlarged; bring me out of my distresses. Look upon my affliction and my trouble, and forgive all my sins.

My Prayer: My troubles are many, Lord. You see my affliction. You see all the difficulties that come along with this life, and You see the suffering of Your children. Show me when these difficulties are a result of my sin and forgive me for them, God. Deliver me in Your time.

Your Prayer:

Psalm 26:11-12 – But as for me, I shall walk in my integrity; redeem me, and be gracious to me. My foot stands on a level place; in the congregations I shall bless the Lord.

My Prayer: God, through all my troubles and the deepest pit of despair, I will walk in my integrity by Your grace. I will serve You through my life and I will not turn from Your ways. Hold me securely on solid ground so that my feet never stumble. Thank You for picking me up when I fall.

Your Prayer:

Apply:

1. Make a list of things that you are waiting for God to do or deliver you from.

2. Evaluate your life and see if there is any sin that needs to be turned from.

3. Pray through these lists and commit to turning from any sin and to waiting for God's perfect timing for deliverance or action.

Memorize:

Psalm 25:4-5 – Make me know Your ways, O Lord; teach me Your paths. Lead me in Your truth and teach me, for You are the God of my salvation; for You I wait all the day.

Journal Additional Prayers and Thoughts

Day 10 – Song of Thanksgiving

Read and Meditate:

Psalm 27:1 – 29:11

Learn:

When I applied to my first college, many years after graduating high school, I accidentally had my high school send my transcripts to me instead of the school. No big deal, they just had to email the school later, but I realized I had never actually seen my transcripts. Well, I graduated with a 3.3 GPA and was ranked 11 out of a class of 20. That was not a surprise, I knew I did not do that well in school, but I thought it was my history and science grades that held me back from a higher standing. I remember working so hard to pass my history and science classes. Well, imagine my surprise when I looked at my transcripts and noticed that the classes that I received the lowest marks in were my music classes! I thought I was good at music! I've been singing specials for church my entire life. One time, I had someone come up to thank me after church and they said, "you are not the best singer in the world, but you sure do have heart." That should have been a clue. I guess I am not nearly as good as I thought I was, so allow me to publicly apologize to anyone who has had to suffer through me singing for Jesus.

Yes, this was eye opening for me. I do not too often sing for church anymore unless I am asked to. I may not be destined to be a professional singer, but I will never stop belting out praises to the Lord. Today's passage is filled with beautiful truths about God's care for us and our response of praise back to Him. We can offer a song of thanksgiving to the Lord no matter our skill level. Do not ever be afraid to sing out during the music time at church. When you are leaning into the Lord during a season of battle or discouragement, it will be a natural reaction to pour out praise to Him with just the right song. Own it! Belt it out, and do not let anyone discourage you in your praise and thanksgiving to the Lord. He is so good to us all the time and He deserves the heartfelt praise of His saints.

Pray:
Psalm 27:3 – Though a host encamp against me, my heart will not fear; though war arise against me, in spite of this I shall be confident.

My Prayer: Dear Lord, the truth is that sometimes I am afraid. When people slander me and lie about me, I worry about the damage it might do. When oppression comes and my mind is attacked on every side, I fear in those moments. Yet, You are there waiting for me to come to You and calm those fears. When I come to Your Word and I talk to You in prayer, the fear goes away and Your truth sustains me. Thank You for Your word and the confidence that You give.

Your Prayer:

Psalm 27:13-14 – I would have despaired unless I had believed that I would see the goodness of the Lord in the land of the living. Wait for the Lord; be strong and let your heart take courage; Yes, wait for the Lord.

My Prayer: Oh God, You are the reason that I do not get overwhelmed in depression. So many things threaten to discourage me. Forgive me for the times I live in discouragement. Forgive me for the times I panic and move ahead of You instead of waiting on You. You are always good, and Your timing is always perfect. Please help me remember this in the day to day moments of life. Thank

You for showing me Your goodness and saving me from despair!

Your Prayer:

Psalm 28:7 – The Lord is my strength and my shield; my heart trusts in Him, and I am helped; therefore my heart exults, and with my song I shall thank Him.

My Prayer: Thank You for always being my strength and my shield! Your strength is what keeps me going through years of struggle and heartache. Without your shield about me, I do not even want to imagine how bad life could get. Thank You for the comfort and protection Your shield offers me. I wake up so often with a song in my heart to You. I love you so much and am so grateful that You have given us music that I can sing my praises to You!

Your Prayer:

Apply:

1. Pick your favorite song that gives total praise to Jesus.

2. Crank it up and belt it out to Him!

3. If you do not already, allow yourself to engage in the singing this Sunday at church. Join the "choir of the saints" as you sing praise and thanksgiving along with your brothers and sisters at your church.

Memorize:

Psalm 28:7 – The Lord is my strength and my shield; my heart trusts in Him, and I am helped; therefore my heart exults, and with my song I shall thank Him.

Journal Additional Prayers and Thoughts

Day 11 – A Walking Target

Read and Meditate:

Psalm 30:1 – 31:24

Learn:

When someone accepts the call of God on his life, he must also accept the fact that a target has been put on his back by the enemy. Satan does not want you to be effective for the Lord, and so there will be forces working against you as you seek to follow the direction of God. David was anointed by God to serve Him by being king of Israel. Before he ever took the throne, David was met with some pretty intense trials. He is known as "a man after God's own heart," yet his life was marked by extreme challenges and opposition. As a result, he faced significant amounts of discouragement and depression.

There is no doubt that a life well-lived for the Lord brings about a certain amount of heart wrenching trials. Throughout our years in ministry my husband and I have both been lied to, lied about, schemed against, slandered, backstabbed, and heartbroken. We have also been used by God to impact the eternal lives of thousands of people over the years. The blessings of ministry do not go unnoticed, and they help fuel our prayers of thanksgiving. However, it is the trials that drive us to our knees, night after night, begging God for wisdom, for strength, and often for rescue. He has shown up in our lives in ways that we would never have been able to imagine. Much like David, we have learned to praise God amid depression. We have learned how to lean into the strength that only comes from God. That is what trials will do for you, if you let them.

Are you struggling through something today? Remember that God is the one who supplies strength in your time of need. He is the only one who can rescue you. He is the source of true joy. Lean into Him as you read today's passage again.

We must also recognize that David never gave up. He wanted to many times. If discouragement has you so weighed down that you feel like giving up, please remember that God wants to rescue you. He desires to give you peace and joy even during your trials. He has a plan that we do not always know about, and we must trust Him. I encourage you to write down today's memory verse and keep it in front of you every day. God is a good, good God and He will not let you down.

Pray:

Psalm 30:5 – For His anger is but for a moment, His favor is for a lifetime; weeping may last for the night, but a shout of joy comes in the morning.

My Prayer: Dear Lord, thank You for not staying angry when I sin. Thank You for Your forgiveness and constant grace. Remind me of Your favor and fill me with Your joy every day!

Your Prayer:

Psalm 31:2-3 – Incline Your ear to me, rescue me quickly; be to me a rock of strength, a stronghold to save me, for You are my rock and my fortress; for Your name's sake You will lead me and guide me.

My Prayer: God, I can do nothing without You. I do not know what direction to take without Your guiding me. I live in emotional chaos when I think too long on my circumstances. I need You, Lord, to be my strength and come to my rescue. I mess things up every time Lord.

Thank You for never giving up on me. Thank You for giving me the strength to get through the trials of both my own making and those that I have no control over.

Your Prayer:

Psalm 31:7-8 – I will rejoice and be glad in Your lovingkindness, because You have seen my affliction; You have known the troubles of my soul, and You have not given me over into the hand of the enemy; You have set my feet in a large place.

My Prayer: I am so grateful that You do not place me on the side of a steep mountain where it is impossible to gain my footing. I feel like that in life sometimes, but when You save me, You place me on solid ground. The place You set me is open, large enough to always find sure footing. Thank You for being so kind to me.

Your Prayer:

Apply:

1. Keep a record of challenges that arise when you are actively serving the Lord.
2. Notice any struggles that repeat often and pray over those areas.
3. If you are struggling so much that you are ready to give up a specific ministry or service, talk to a trusted Pastor or biblical counselor today.

Memorize:

Psalm 31: 14-15a – But as for me, I trust in You, O Lord, I say, "You are my God." My times are in Your hand;

Journal Additional Prayers and Thoughts

.

Day 12 – The Great Perspective Shift

Read and Meditate:

Psalm 32:1 – 34:22

Learn:

How do you measure blessings? When you look at your life and the lives of those around you, do you consider some people to be more blessed than others? Are there times in life that you would say you are greatly blessed, but other times that you feel like blessing is scarce? From our perspective, the more a person has, the more blessed they are. We measure blessing by success, relationships, and material gain. My husband and children are blessings from the Lord. He has blessed me with gifts to serve Him as well as skills and talents that produce income for the needs of our household. Over the years, there have been times when the blessings are overflowing, and there have been other times where it takes a great deal of effort to see any blessings at all. Why is it that we tend to look at blessing from the perspective of material gain?

Let me introduce you to the great perspective shift offered to us in today's passage. There are four verses scattered through the Psalmist's writing that we would do well to pay attention to. They teach us a lot about how we ought to recognize and measure blessing in our life.

Psalm 32:1 – *"How blessed is he whose transgression is forgiven, whose sin is covered*!" Have your sins been covered by the blood of Jesus Christ? What other blessing could you possibly need than to know that you are forgiven of all your sins by the almighty God?

Psalm 32:2 – *"How blessed is the man to whom the Lord does not impute iniquity, and in whose spirit there is no deceit*!" Not only does God forgive our sins, but He does not even hold a record of them. That word "impute" means to put on one's account. He says that once we are forgiven, we owe nothing for those sins. What a blessing!

Psalm 33:12 – *"Blessed is the nation whose God is the Lord, the people whom He has chosen for His own inheritance."* If you are born-again, it is because God chose you and drew you to Himself. You are so blessed to be a child of God, chosen to be grafted into His family as a son or daughter and joint heir with Jesus Christ.

Psalm 34:8 – *"O taste and see that the Lord is good; How blessed is the man who takes refuge in Him*!" You see, our blessing is not the "stuff" that God gives. Our blessing is God Himself!

We are already blessed to the fullest measure the second we become a believer. Psalm 34:1-3 gives us a better perspective. We are to turn around and bless the Lord with our praise, brag on the Lord and bring others along to exalt His holy name. Do you need a perspective shift today? As you pray through a few sections from today's passage, remember how blessed you truly are.

Pray:
Psalm 32:3-4 – Sing to Him a new song; play skillfully with a shout of joy. For the word of the Lord is upright, and all His work is done in faithfulness.

My Prayer: Thank You, Lord, for always being faithful in everything You do. I am so blessed by You. Thank You for Your word that reminds me of the proper perspective and keeps my heart fixed on You and Your greatness.

Your Prayer:
Psalm 34:9-10 – O fear the Lord, you His saints; for to those who fear Him there is no want. The young lions do lack and suffer hunger; but they who seek the Lord shall not be in want of any good thing.

My Prayer: God, You always provide for every one of my needs. I sometimes get caught up in the materialism of this world and forget that I do not need any of earth's treasures. I have never gone without a single need. You have always provided, and for that I am so grateful. Thank You for keeping Your heavenly perspective in front of me.

Your Prayer:

Psalm 34:19 – Many are the afflictions of the righteous, but the Lord delivers him out of them all.

My Prayer: I have found this verse to be so true in my life. The afflictions are many. They are often overwhelming. I find myself falling into the trap of discouragement more often than I should. Then, You remind me that You have always delivered me from every affliction and You will remain faithful, even now. Thank You for your love, Your provision, and Your faithfulness. I love You so much!

Your Prayer:

Apply:

Do you have the proper perspective yet? All you need to consider yourself blessed is your salvation. Anything else beyond that is an added blessing that is never promised.

1. With that in mind, make a list of all your "other" blessings. They are all around you, every day.

2. Take time to thank God for each of these blessings. Talk about them often to remain in the proper perspective.

3. Who can you bring along to exalt the Lord? Find someone to share your joy in the Lord with today.

Memorize:

Psalm 34:8 – O taste and see that the Lord is good; how blessed is the man who takes refuge in Him.

Journal Additional Prayers and Thoughts

Day 13 – Cultivating Faithfulness

Read and Meditate:

Psalm 35:1 – 37:40

Learn:

You might notice that David asks the Lord quite often to have vengeance on his enemies. This passage is no different as he begins by asking God to contend and fight for him. Possibly, David knew something that we all should learn. God fights our battles so much better than we can.

When we try to fight back against people who are clearly attacking us, it only escalates the situation and causes more pain. God knows all the details of the situation. He might not rise up right away and vindicate the faithful, but He always makes the right decisions in the right timing. Even though David wondered where God was and why He was not defeating these evil men, he continued to give thanks and praise to the Lord. This is a practice that we would all do well to adopt in our own lives.

David advises in Psalm 37 that we ought not lose our temper because of evildoers. When we get angry and start lashing out, it always makes matters worse. The best way to handle it is to wait on the Lord, for however long it takes. Now, he does not just give the blanket statement to "wait" without also telling us how to accomplish this task. Psalm 37:3-5 tells us exactly what we should be doing while we wait, even during impossible circumstances.

We are to trust, dwell, cultivate, delight, commit, and rest. We trust God no matter what. We do not have to necessarily enjoy the circumstance, but we should trust God and His timing. We are to dwell in His presence as we cultivate faithfulness in our lives. Dwelling takes time and commitment. Cultivating takes hard work. We must spend ample time with the Lord, learning His word and communicating with Him.

As we trust Him and spend time building a relationship with Him, we begin to delight in Him. He becomes our greatest joy and passion. When the psalmist says, "He will give you the desires of your heart", it means that as you develop your walk with God, He begins to change your desires to line up with His own heart. It is at this point that we become capable of committing our way to the Lord. Once we are fully committed, we rest. When we trust Him, and we spend our days with Him, and we are committed to His way alone, then we can enjoy the most beautiful rest as we patiently wait for His will in His timing.

Pray:

Psalm 35:1-2 – Contend, O Lord, with those who contend with me; fight against those who fight against me, take hold of buckler and shield and rise up for my help.

My Prayer: Dear God, let me always remember to let You fight my battles for me. You are The Almighty. Rise up against those who try to destroy the work You have called us to do.

Your Prayer:

Psalm 37:3-5 – Trust in the Lord and do good; dwell in the land and cultivate faithfulness. Delight yourself in the Lord; and He will give you the desires of your heart. Commit your way to the Lord, trust also in Him and He will do it.

My Prayer: Thank You, Lord, for putting Your desires in my heart. I do trust You and work to grow in faithfulness and relationship to You. I am still so far from being where I know I should be; where You desire me to be. Forgive my laziness. Help me learn more and more how to cultivate faithfulness and fully commit to You.

Your Prayer:

Psalm 37:23-24 – The steps of a man are established by the Lord, and He delights in his way. When he falls, he will not be hurled headlong, because the Lord is the One who holds his hand.

My Prayer: God, I feel so incredibly loved and protected by You knowing that You are holding my hand. Just as I held the hands of my children when they were learning to walk, You gently lead me with the comfort of Your Fatherly hold. Thank You for not letting me go when I fall. Help me feel the gentle tug of Your hand when You say, "it is time to go this way now." You are such a good Father, Lord God.

Your Prayer:

Apply:

1. Make a list of ways that you can continue to cultivate faithfulness in your life. Some suggestions could be attending a Bible Study, joining a Life Group at your church, setting aside a special time every day to spend with the Lord, adding Scripture memory to your daily life, etc.

2. Now choose one thing from your list and start it!

Memorize:

Psalm 35:18 – I will give You thanks in the great congregation; I will praise You among a mighty throng.

Journal Additional Prayers and Thoughts

Day 14 – The Gravity of Sin

Read and Meditate:

Psalm 38:1 – Psalm 39:13

Learn:

Why do we not look at our sin more seriously? Why do we live as if God just winks and looks the other way when we ignore His commands and do our own thing? Since we live in a post-resurrection world, we can receive the beautiful gift of God's grace when we come to Christ at Salvation. Grace is an undeserved miracle that often is grossly underestimated. Most Christians do not really understand the magnitude of God's grace simply because they refuse to acknowledge the gravity of their sin. David not only recognized his sin, but he also accepted his place before God and the response of God to his sin.

We have tried so hard to make sure new believers feel loved and accepted by God, that we are failing to teach the seriousness of sinful behavior. God is the same yesterday, today, and tomorrow. Just because He has freely given us grace and forgiveness for our sin does not mean that He ignores our future sin. Sin still makes God angry. Surely from the unsaved, who the Bible refers to as "the wicked" or "the world", but even more so from the born-again believers. Think about it. When someone wrongs you in some way, does it not hurt worse coming from a close friend or family member than it does from that guy you barely know? All sin angers the Lord, but as Christians we must never confuse grace for a free pass for the next time we sin.

David understood this, and he spends most of these two chapters explaining just how devesting sin is in the life of a child of God. When a Christian lives with unconfessed sin, it produces anxiety, depression, physical pain and suffering, and a big strain in his relationship with the Lord. It would do us well to take today as an opportunity to do some serious soul searching and honestly evaluate our life before our God.

Pray:
Psalm 38:3-4 – There is no soundness in my flesh because of Your indignation; there is no health in my bones because of my sin. For my iniquities are gone over my head; as a heavy burden they weigh too much for me.

My Prayer: God, I have felt this pain all too often in my lifetime. Thank You for allowing me to suffer so that I recognize when I am sinning against You. Thank You for giving me Your Spirit to convict me and for bringing me back into a healthy place when I repent. Forgive even my unknown sins that might be causing weight on my life right now. Please keep me sensitive to hear Your conviction.

Your Prayer:

Psalm 39:4-5 – Lord, make me to know my end and what is the extent of my days; let me know how transient I am. Behold, You have made my days as handbreadths, and my lifetime as nothing in Your sight; surely every man at his best is a mere breath.

My Prayer: Dear Lord, You alone know the number of my days and the events that my lifetime will hold. In light of eternity, my short life on earth is just a momentary journey. Life here is fleeting, and I desire to live it with eternity in mind. Help me recognize every mission, every calling, every service You would have me do throughout the rest of my life. Equip me for Your work, make it known to me, and remind me often that my life here is short. Thank You so much that You have put eternity in my heart and that this life will not be the end! Help me keep this perspective as I continue to follow Your direction.

Your Prayer:

Psalm 39:7-8 – And now, Lord, for what do I wait? My hope is in You. Deliver me from all my transgressions; make me not the reproach of the foolish.

My Prayer: All my hope is in You alone. My life is in Your mighty hands and I will wait on You to do whatever You will with my life every day. Help me stay out of sinful attitudes so that I might be a good testimony for You. Forgive me when I fall and use me however You see fit.

Your Prayer:

Apply:

1. What sins are you ignoring in your life? Search your heart and ask God to reveal any area of sin that you have been ignoring or justifying.

2. Write down whatever attitudes, actions, or avoidances the Holy Spirit brings to your mind.

3. Confess these sins to the Lord and ask Him to forgive you.

4. Find someone you trust who will hold you accountable to change this area of your life. Admit the sin to this person and ask them to confront you when they notice it in your life.

Memorize:

Psalm 38:15 – For I hope in You, O Lord; You will answer, O Lord my God.

Journal Additional Prayers and Thoughts

Day 15 – Despaired or Dehydrated?

Read and Meditate:

Psalm 40:1 – Psalm 42:11

Learn:

No one is immune from feelings of despair and discouragement. I have always cherished Psalm 42:1, "*As the deer pants for the water brooks, so my soul pants for God, for the living God.*" I have quoted this verse since grade school and even learned some very beautiful songs to express this powerful verse. I used to associate this verse with that of a healthy believer who does not have any discouragement or hinderances. I also used to define a "healthy" believer as one who is strong in faith and lacking any kind of discouragement. It was not until my adult years that my eyes were opened to the context of this entire chapter and I realized my understanding of a "healthy" believer was wrong.

Today's passage is one that was written by the sons of Korah, likely during the time when they were running and hiding with David from his son, Absolam. Enemies were after the king, everyone was scared and discouraged, and life was not at all normal. The sons of Korah could be compared to the worship pastor's, choirs, and praise teams of today. They were responsible for leading the people of God into meaningful worship, primarily through song. They used to have a very fulfilling ministry as the worship leaders, but at the time of this Psalm they were not able to fulfill their role. As a result, they felt lost and discouraged. They were losing heart fast and desperately wanted to get back to the mission that God had placed in their heart.

Through tears and discouragement, these sons of Korah learned a very valuable lesson. While their despair stemmed from fear and a type of identity loss, they quickly realized that it was not the service they were really missing. They desperately missed God Himself and the closeness they felt during their worship. In a time of complete loss and desperate lifestyle upset, these men expressed their deep desire to be in the presence of their God.

When I am dried up, lost, searching for hope, discouraged by impossible circumstances, then I understand what it means to thirst for the Lord. It is not a feeling that you can manufacture. Rather, it is an automatic reaction of the believer who finds themselves in a tough circumstance. It shows up in our life as discouragement, anxiety, tears, depression, despair. Those feelings are not evil, they are clues that your soul is desperately thirsty for the presence of God. You are not really in despair. You are in fact, dehydrated for the Lord. So, we open our Bibles to hear from Him and we open our mouths to speak with Him. Are you discouraged? Spend some time in His presence today!

Pray:

Psalm 40:9-10 – I have proclaimed glad tidings of righteousness in the great congregation; Behold, I will not restrain my lips, O Lord, You know. I have not hidden Your righteousness within my heart; I have spoken of Your faithfulness and Your salvation; I have not concealed Your lovingkindness and Your truth from the great congregation.

My Prayer: Lord God, I will not keep my mouth shut about Your righteousness and Your faithfulness. I will sing of Your greatness, and I will speak of Your ways. I pray that You give me opportunities clearly and plainly where I can share You and the gospel of Jesus Christ with the world around me.

Your Prayer:

Psalm 42:1-2 – As the deer pants for the water brooks, so my soul pants for You, O God. My soul thirsts for God, for the living God; When shall I come and appear before God?

My Prayer: Oh God, You are my sustainer. You are the only One who can quench the thirst of my longing. Every discouragement and every fear leads me to Your feet, O Lord. Thank You for the trials in my life that remind me how desperately I need You every day. I thirst for You and I long to be with You soon.

Your Prayer:

Psalm 42:5;11 – Why are you in despair, O my soul? And why have you become disturbed within me? Hope in God, for I shall again praise Him for the help of His presence. Why are you in despair, O my soul? And why have you become disturbed within me? Hope in God, for I shall yet praise Him. The help of my countenance and my God.

My Prayer: God, I love how close You are that I can always come to You and hope in You when I am in despair. Thank You for hearing me and helping me. God, it is so amazing that You allow us to see the progression from being in Your presence to having a changed appearance. As I spend time with You, my countenance changes and others notice. When I neglect You, people notice that, too. Lord, thank You for being so real and so good to me.

Your Prayer:

Apply:

1. Make a list of the things that are weighing you down today. What is causing you anxiety or discouragement?
2. Take those specific things to the Lord and thank Him for His presence that fills you with hope.
3. Remember that you have direct access to the presence of God anytime you want. Do not take it for granted.

Memorize:

Psalm 42:1 – As the deer pants for the water brooks, so my soul pants for You, O God.

Journal Additional Prayers and Thoughts

Day 16 – God is in Control, Even of the Crisis

Read and Meditate:

Psalm 43:1 – Psalm 45:17

Learn:

God is sovereign. This means that God can do what He wants, when He wants, to whomever He wants at any given time. Often, He provides very generously both in materials and circumstances and it is in these times of comfort that we find it easy to serve the Lord faithfully. There are other times, however, that He allows us to go through intense struggle. These times might leave us feeling like we are crushed under the weight of God's sovereignty. So, how do you respond to these times, knowing that they have been allowed by God?

Well, you will notice in today's passage that the sons of Korah found themselves feeling crushed and rejected by God. They loved the Lord! We saw yesterday that they longed to get back to the place of feeling His presence in their life. As they reflect upon all they know about their God, they remember all the wonderful works that He has done. They heard how He parted the Red Sea so that His people could escape from Egypt. They heard how He made the sun stand still for hours while Joshua finished winning a battle. They knew all the miracles and they praised Him for all He had done. Now, they found themselves in a dire situation and they faced a choice of how they would respond. Here is what they chose:

- They recognized that God allowed this. They acknowledge God's authority, not in a blaming way, but rather as simply a matter of fact. God is God and He can allow what He wants, when He wants. They believed and accepted this truth.

- They remembered their place of service before the Lord. They focused on the greatness of God and expressed to Him that they knew He was fully capable of saving them, if that was His will. They trusted in His sovereignty and they did not fall away from His truth.

- They asked for help. Knowing He is in control, knowing He is capable, and trusting in His will, they begged the Lord to rise up and save them.

Think about the last time you went through a major crisis in your life. You might be in one now. Do you believe that God allowed this crisis? How does your response to the crisis match up with what God teaches in today's passage?

Pray:

Psalm 43:3 – O send out Your light and Your truth, let them lead me; let them bring me to Your holy hill and to Your dwelling places.

My Prayer: Dear Lord, I need Your truth and Your light to guide me. Sometimes, the path in front of me seems so dark. I only want to go where You lead and where You guide, so reveal my next steps. Please make Your steps clear so that there is no doubt that they are from You.

Your Prayer:

Psalm 44:1 – O God, we have heard with our ears, our fathers have told us the work that You did in their days, in the days of old.

My Prayer: Thank You, Lord, for recording so many of Your amazing wonders in the Bible. Learning about all the supernatural things You have done gives me such peace for my life. There is nothing too difficult for You. You are the God of the impossible.

Your Prayer:

Psalm 44:17-19 – All this has come upon us, but we have not forgotten You, and we have not dealt falsely with Your covenant. Our heart has not turned back, and our steps have not deviated from Your way, yet You have crushed us in a place of jackals and covered us with the shadow of death.

My Prayer: Lord God, I do not always understand why You allow certain things to happen. Sometimes, You guide in a direction that ends up crushing us. Lord, help me to remember that life is not about me and that You are the sovereign God. Your plan is always best and always serves a purpose, even when it hurts.

Your Prayer:

Apply:

1. Make a list of times in the past that were difficult to get through.

2. Record how God took you through those times.

3. If you are in a crisis now, spend some time in specific prayer to God. Lay out all the details of your situation and commit to trusting Him no matter the outcome.

Memorize:

Psalm 44:18 – Our heart has not turned back, and our steps have not deviated from Your way.

Journal Additional Prayers and Thoughts

Day 17 – God Most High

Read and Meditate:

Psalm 46:1 – Psalm 48:14

Learn:

Did you ever play "king of the mountain" when you were younger? It has been banned from school yards for decades because it is too rough for kids to play today. We usually played during the winter when the snow mounds were taller than our teachers and we were bundled up like fluffy marshmallows in our snow pants and winter coats. The object of the game is to stay at the top of the hill the longest without being knocked off. Each child would have the chance to wrestle or shove the "king" off the hill. If unsuccessful, the king would hold onto his title, but if the king was knocked down then the assailant would now become king of the mountain. You can see why it has been banned. Everyone wanted to be king!

Today's reading points us to another King. God of Jacob, the Lord Most High. He is the King over all the earth. Much like the game mentioned above, many have tried to overthrow God from His throne. They wrestle and grapple with Him, trying to elevate their own thoughts and their own ways. The difference with God as King is that no one will ever be successful in overthrowing Him from His throne. Even if we think that we are sitting on the throne of our own lives by disregarding God's rule and living our own way, we only deceive ourselves. God is always on the throne; He is always in control. This gives us great comfort when we are confronted with disaster and conflict.

The Psalmist recognizes the power of God and gives us several truths that we need to believe. First, we can be fearless amidst a world of change. When it seems like evil is succeeding, we can remember that God cannot be knocked off His throne. Second, God is the ruler of the nations and one day every person will recognize it. He is the only true help in times of trouble because He alone knows all the details of this world. Third, God is the one who should be feared. Human fear causes conflict and strife as we react to our circumstances out of anxiety and false emotions. Godly fear reminds us that nothing can happen outside of God's control, so we quit striving against the things of this world and return our focus to living a godly life as He directs. God is King and thus is the only source of help and strength that we need.

Pray:

Psalm 46:1-2 God is our refuge and strength, A very present help in trouble. Therefore we will not fear, though the earth should change and though the mountains slip into the heart of the sea;

My Prayer: You are my refuge and strength. You are here, actively helping me in my trouble. Thank You for being my help every day. Thank You for giving me the peace and confidence to walk through this dark world knowing that You are in control and I have no reason to fear. Even if the unimaginable happens, I will not fear for I know that You are the Most High. I trust Your good will no matter what.

Your Prayer:

Psalm 46:10-11 Cease striving and know that I am God; I will be exalted among the nations, I will be exalted in the earth. The Lord of hosts is with us; The God of Jacob is our stronghold.

My Prayer: Lord, I do not want to be just another voice arguing over things that mean nothing in the scheme of eternity. You alone will triumph over every nation. Show me how to cease striving and how You would have me speak to glorify You alone.

Your Prayer:

Psalm 47:1-2 O Clap your hands, all peoples; Shout to God with the voice of joy, For the Lord Most High is to be feared, A great King over all the earth.

My Prayer: I am overjoyed, dear Lord, at the thought of You. You are a great King; You are THE Great King! I do not understand all the details about Your Kingdom, but I look forward to the day that it is here forever, and this earth is done away. Thank You for Your Word and the hope it brings as I learn to fear You more and more.

Your Prayer:

Apply:

What are you afraid of? Wars? Terrorism? Crime? The political atmosphere? Change?

1. Make a list of the things that cause fear to invade your heart.

2. Examine this list in the context of today's reading.

3. Ask God to help you overcome the fear of these things as you submit to His authority as God Most High.

Memorize:

Psalm 46:1-2a – God is our refuge and strength, a very present help in trouble. Therefore we will not fear, though the earth should change…

Journal Additional Prayers and Thoughts

Day 18 – Hidden Sin

Read and Meditate:

Psalm 49:1 – Psalm 51:19

Learn:

Psalm 51 was written by David after his affair with Bathsheba. It is a beautiful Psalm that reveals a sincere heart of repentance. We have much to learn from David about our own sin and need for forgiveness. I encourage you to read the whole story in 2 Samuel 11-12 and then re-read Psalm 51. Here is a quick overview.

There were many sins that led David to the point of sleeping with Bathsheba, and there were many more sins after the fact. When he found out that Bathsheba was pregnant with his child, he began to attempt a cover up. He brought her husband home from war, in hopes that he would assume the child was his. This attempt failed when Uriah proved to have greater honor than his king. He refused to sleep with his wife while everyone else was at war. David's sin continued when he orchestrated a way to kill Uriah, making it appear as a casualty of war. When he heard that the job was done and Uriah was dead, he quickly married Bathsheba so that everyone would view him as a hero and assume the pregnancy was one of honor. Yes, David's sins were many, and as far as David knew, they were secret.

King David, the man after God's own heart, thought that he could go on living in sin so long as no one found out about it. He justified his actions to himself, continuing to live one lie after another. He was not concerned with how his actions would affect anyone else, including Bathsheba. How often do we make choices that we know are wrong, but justify them with false pretenses? How often do we act as though God does not see?

David assumed that he had gotten away with his sin. He quickly learned, as we must, that our sin is never hidden from God. He sees all and He knows your heart. There is a great need for brokenness in our repentance and the amazing grace of God as He forgives. God desires a broken spirit and complete truth, even in the innermost part of your heart.

As you pray through today's passage, be truthful with God about your sin. He already knows it anyway. Think about the sins you might be hiding from others. Maybe, you are hiding sin from yourself. Do you push away conviction by justifying your actions and thoughts? Take it to the Lord in brokenness and repent!

Pray:

Psalm 49:7-8 – No man can by any means redeem his brother or give to God a ransom for Him – For the redemption of his soul is costly, and he should cease trying forever –

My Prayer: Lord God, it is so easy to forget that my "free gift" was not free at all. Redemption is costly, it cost You Your Son. Thank You for suffering, thank You for giving it all up for me. I wish I could force people to salvation, but I know that they must choose. Thank You for Your gift of salvation. Help me share it well with all those who think that their good works are enough to pay the price.

Your Prayer:

Psalm 51:1 – Be gracious to me, O God, according to Your lovingkindness; According to the greatness of Your compassion blot out my transgressions.

My Prayer: I am such a wretched sinner, Lord. I am so grateful that You deal graciously with me; not dependent on my actions, but according to Your mercy. Forgive me of my many sins Lord, the ones I know and the ones I am overlooking.

Your Prayer:

Psalm 51:6;10 – Behold, You desire truth in the innermost being, and in the hidden part You will make me know wisdom…. Create in me a clean heart, O God, and renew a steadfast spirit within me.

My Prayer: Search my heart, O God. I cannot hide anything from You and I do not even want to try. Know my heart, reveal my sin, and create newness in me every day. Give me a heart like Yours, God – Steadfast, wise, clean. I cannot change my own heart, so I am asking for Your help to create a new heart in me as You make me more and more like Your Son.

Your Prayer:

Apply:

1. What sin are you consciously hiding? Are you broken by this sin?
2. Bring it into the light by confessing it to the Lord.
3. Share it with your pastor or trusted Christian mentor who will be able to hold you accountable in this area.

Memorize:

Psalm 51:12 – Restore to me the joy of Your salvation and sustain me with a willing spirit.

Journal Additional Prayers and Thoughts

Day 19 – Never Good Enough

Read and Meditate:

Psalm 52:1 – Psalm 53:6

Learn:

In my early years of parenting I sought out as much advice and counsel as I could get. Christian conferences, books, Bible studies – I soaked it all in. I did not agree with everything, and I learned to be discerning with what I heard. I do not remember where I heard it, but a very common teaching on parenting is the idea of good vs bad. The premise was that we should never tell our child "that was bad" or "you were bad" when they disobeyed. The reasoning had everything to do with the self-esteem and confidence of the child. We do not want them to think that they are bad, only that the action was naughty.

While we did adopt this practice into our parenting, we changed it slightly to better match up with Scripture. My husband and I decided not to use the word "bad", but we also would not use the word "good" in these instances. Instead, we chose the words "sin", "obey", and "disobey" in our discipline or teaching moments. The reason is clear as you read today's passage.

"God has looked down from heaven upon the sons of men to see if there is anyone who understands, who seeks after God. Every one of them has turned aside; together they have become corrupt; there is no one who does good, not even one." Psalm 53:2-3

God says that no one is good. No one does good. I might think that I am a good person. In human terms, I am a good person. I read my Bible, go to church, and help others. I do not cuss, get drunk, or gamble. I am a faithful wife, mother, and friend. I obey the Lord as He teaches me how to live. Yet, all these things do not make me good in God's eyes. When I compare my "goodness" to the goodness and holiness of God I am still light years below Him. Therefore, I need grace. As a born-again Christian, God now looks at me through the blood of Jesus Christ and He sees good. Not my good, but Christ's good.

We have nothing to boast about in ourselves, even on our best day. We must acknowledge that we are not good, and that means that we are, in fact, bad at the core of our humanity. We will never be good enough. It is only through Christ that God can look down on us and see good.

If you believe that you are good, and you are trusting in your goodness to get you to heaven, I beg you to take another look at the "how to become a Christian" section printed in the back of this book before you finish today's devotional time. It is literally a matter of life and death!

Pray:

Psalm 52:1 – Why do you boast in evil, O mighty man? The lovingkindness of God endures all day long.

My Prayer: God, thank You for Your lovingkindness. Forgive me when I boast in earthly things. Help me focus on Your mercies and Your holiness. The world boasts of wealth, success, and prosperity. Create a heart of humility within me that only boasts in the greatness of Your works.

Your Prayer:

Psalm 52:7; 53:1 – Behold, the man who would not make God his refuge, But trusted in the abundance of his riches and was strong in his evil desires . . . The fool has said in his heart, "There is no God," They are corrupt and have committed abominable injustice; There is no one who does good.

My Prayer: We have all been this fool, O God. Thank You for saving me even though I am not good, and I have not always trusted You. Please work in the hearts of those who are still in this foolish place of rejecting You. Help them to understand and accept Your grace.

Your Prayer:

Psalm 52:8-9 – But as for me, I am like a green olive tree in the house of God; I trust in the lovingkindness of God forever and ever. I will give You thanks forever, because You have done it, and I will wait on Your name, for it is good, in the presence of Your godly ones.

My Prayer: I am only blessed because You have allowed it. I am only saved because of Your grace. You have set me apart and caused me to grow in You. Thank You for saving me and for showing mercy on me every day.

Your Prayer:

Apply:

Find a way to proclaim God's goodness today. Here are some ideas to get you started.

1. Call a friend and tell them something you are currently thankful for.
2. Choose one attribute of God and brag on Him about it though social media.
3. Share your testimony of salvation with someone.
4. Write a poem or a blog post about how God has blessed you lately.

Memorize:

Psalm 52:8b – I trust in the lovingkindness of God forever and ever.

Journal Additional Prayers and Thoughts

Day 20 – Toxic People

Read and Meditate:

Psalm 54:1 – 55:23

Learn:

The word "toxic" has become a growing trend in our world today. Everywhere we turn we are told to get rid of anything toxic from our life. The end goal of this philosophy is that you become as happy and stress free as possible. It has even spilled over into how we categorize people. If someone causes you too much anxiety, they are toxic and must be avoided.

While it all sounds so good, especially while scrolling through thousands of memes on Facebook, it is not biblical. Are there people God tells us to avoid? Yes. Are there people who are truly toxic that require some type of action to set up boundaries with? Yes. However, they are few and far between. Not everyone who makes poor choices is toxic.

David understood how it felt to have truly toxic people in his life. King Saul was unstable at best, a complete sociopath at worst. He allowed sin to get in his life and he refused to align his life with God's will. The result was a damaged mind and troubled spirit. He worked up imaginations that David was somehow a threat to him and his kingdom, and he acted on those false feelings. Saul began hunting David like an animal, sending him into hiding. David got through that season, never once disrespecting or slandering King Saul. Later, he takes another hit from his own son and his trusted counselor.

Long story short, David's son Absalom kills his brother Amnon in revenge for raping their sister. Absalom goes into hiding for a time and when he comes back, he conspires along with Ahithophel, David's counselor, to take over the kingdom. He succeeds, sending David back into hiding as Absalom poses a big threat to his own father. NOW THAT IS TOXIC!

It was likely during this time of running from Absalom that Psalm 55 was written, although it is the same sentiment he had during his time running from Saul. David knew toxic people and he gives us a beautiful Psalm to teach us how the Christian should respond to truly toxic people in our life.

As you meditate on today's passage, notice specifically how David talks about his circumstances and how he deals with his complaints.

Pray:

Psalm 55:12-14 – For it is not an enemy who reproaches me, then I could bear it; nor is it one who hates me who has exalted himself against me, then I could hide myself from him. But it is you, a man my equal, my companion and my familiar friend; we who had sweet fellowship together walked in the house of God in the throng.

My Prayer: Lord, how hard it is when someone close to us hurts us. Remind me that it is only because there is great love there that it hurts so bad. Help me desire restoration and repentance rather than vengeance and bitterness. Help me remember Your example of forgiveness, mercy, and grace.

Your Prayer:

Psalm 55:16-17 – As for me, I shall call upon God, and the Lord will save me. Evening and morning and at noon, I will complain and murmur, and He will hear me.

My Prayer: My complaint comes to You God. Thank You for hearing me and allowing me to bring my troubles to You all day long. Thank You for not pushing me aside as if my concerns are not valid or important. Thank You for always hearing me.

Your Prayer:

Psalm 55:22-23 – Cast your burden upon the Lord and He will sustain you; He will never allow the righteous to be shaken. But You, O God, will bring them down to the pit of destruction; men of bloodshed and deceit will not live out half their days. But I will trust in You.

My Prayer: My trust is always and only in You! You alone sustain me. I do not know what will come of those who fight against me, who are truly toxic to me, but I do know that You lift me up and keep my heart above the pain that these people cause.

Your Prayer:

Apply:

1. Make a list of everyone who you feel is "toxic" in your life.
2. Pray through your list, asking for wisdom to discern which are truly toxic and which just made poor choices.
3. Choose to forgive them.
4. Identify one or two from your list who are not truly toxic but require restoration. Pray about your next steps and make plans to restore the relationship.
5. Identify one or two from your list who are truly toxic. Set up boundaries as necessary. Forgive them and pray for God to deal with their hearts as you release the burden you have carried from them.

Memorize:

Psalm 55:22 – Cast your burden upon the Lord and He will sustain you: He will never allow the righteous to be shaken.

Journal Additional Prayers and Thoughts

Day 21 – God is FOR ME!

Read and Meditate:

Psalm 56:1 – Psalm 57:11

Learn:

Do not be afraid. Some form of this command is spoken in Scripture over three hundred times. God knows how naturally fearful we are as humans. Sometimes, fear is present in the face of real danger. More often, however, fear overtakes us in the form of worry and anxiety about an unrealistic perception. It is in these times of fear that we might feel as if even God is against us. Let me assure you, He is for you, not against you!

When the world seems to be against us, we become afraid of how it will affect our lives. The young mom who sets her expectations on a perfect, story-book life ahead of her feels defeated by fear as those expectations quickly crumble around her. We are afraid for the future of our children if we perceive that we have made mistakes as parents. Fear grips our hearts if we think too long about all the ways our careers could be ruined. Fear comes in many forms, for various reasons, and has the power to paralyze us if we do not respond to it properly.

When we allow fear to rule our heart, we become anxious and stuck. Fear will keep us from serving the Lord. Fear will rob us of healthy relationships. Fear will steal our joy. It is for these reasons, and many more, that we must learn how to deal with fear in our lives.

There are only two choices when we are faced with fear. The wrong choice is to dwell on the fear, thinking about every horrifying scenario that could come from the situation. When we choose to entertain our fears, we quickly become slaves to anxiety which will then lead to depression. The right choice is to trust God. This choice requires more than a quick prayer of asking God to take the fear. In order to trust God, we must know God. We must build a relationship with Him and learn about the attributes that make Him trustworthy.

The only way to learn about God and to grow in relationship with God is to read and study His Word. The more we know Him, the deeper we trust Him. It takes time and effort to develop the kind of relationship with God that trusts Him when we are afraid.

What kind of relationship do you think the Psalmist had with the Lord? What kind of relationship do you currently have with Him? Meditate on today's passage as you examine your own heart response to fear; realizing that God is for you, not against you.

Pray:

Psalm 56:3-4 – When I am afraid, I will put my trust in You. In God, whose word I praise, In God I have put my trust; I shall not be afraid. What can mere man do to me?

My Prayer: Lord, my fears are many, and I trust You with them all. You alone are completely trustworthy, and You alone can handle my fears. I trust You no matter what the outcome, because You know what is best in every circumstance.

Your Prayer:

Psalm 56:8-9 – You have taken account of my wanderings; Put my tears in Your bottle. Are they not in Your book? Then my enemies will turn back in the day when I call; This I know, that God is for me.

My Prayer: These verses are especially sweet to me in this season, O God. I have shed many tears and You have seen them all. I take great comfort in knowing that You hold on to my tears. Thank You for loving me and cherishing me. I am overwhelmed to think that You are for me. I do not deserve Your love and yet You lavish it on me in so many ways. Thank You for loving me!

Your Prayer:

Psalm 57:7 – My heart is steadfast, O God, my heart is steadfast; I will sing, yes, I will sing praises!

My Prayer: My heart is steadfast! Lord, there are times that I cannot claim this statement. Thank You for the work that You have done in my heart that I can truly say that I have a steadfast heart toward You. When I falter, bring me to my senses quickly.

Your Prayer:

Apply:

What are your fears? What do you feel threatened by?

1. Take time to write down the things that worry you and pray about them. Ask God to illuminate these verses as you turn your worries over to Him.

2. Evaluate where your relationship is with the Lord.

3. Make one change that will draw you closer to Him than you are right now. Maybe you can join a Bible Study, set aside more time each day for your devotions with God, increase your tithe to build your faith, or join a ministry team at your church. Maybe you need to commit to joining a church. There are many things that will help you know God better!

Memorize:

Psalm 56:9b – This I know, that God is for me.

Journal Additional Prayers and Thoughts

Day 22 – Justice will be Served

Read and Meditate:

Psalm 58:1 – Psalm 59:17

Learn:

A quick survey through world news will reveal that evil truly does exist. Mass shootings, human trafficking, and terrorism are just a few of the ongoing displays of evil in our world. There are many who practice wickedness in whom is no righteousness at all. The news can be very overwhelming to watch at times.

David was often faced with wicked opposition. By now you should have realized that David was not shy about sharing his emotions with the Lord. He has some strong words and requests about his enemies in today's passage. He is faced with some of the same evil that we see today and is rightly outraged as we should be. The question is, what do we do with that outrage?

David shows us that it is necessary to pour our hearts out to the Lord. Even when our hearts are darkened by revenge and hateful thoughts toward our enemies, we can still bring our thoughts and emotions to God. He is the one who judges, and He is the one who will punish evil. He does this in His way and in His time, which does not always match up with our timing. Evil will be done away with, and those who practice evil will be judged for all eternity.

As we continue through this journey of life, it is vital that we remember the end of the evil man. Justice does not always come on this earth. We live in a fallen world where evil seems to prevail, but there is coming a day when all will be brought to light. Every evil act will receive judgement. The righteous – those who are covered by the blood of Christ – will be rewarded and live with the Lord forever. The wicked – those who do not know the salvation of the Lord – will spend eternity in the Lake of Fire, a far greater judgement than anything they would receive on earth. This should drive us to our knees in prayer. Pray for God to fight against evil. Pray for our hearts to not become discouraged or embittered when it seems that evil is winning. Pray for the souls of men.

Pray:
Psalm 58:11 – And men will say, "Surely there is a reward for the righteous; Surely there is a God who judges on earth!"

My Prayer: God, I cannot wait for the day when all men will know that You are God. It is difficult to see so much evil in the world. It is so discouraging to be met with rejection when I share about You. Help me to live in humility and compassion toward the lost, remembering that it is you who judge.

Your Prayer:

Psalm 59:10 – My God in His lovingkindness will meet me; God will let me look triumphantly upon my foes.

My Prayer: I do not have enemies the way David did, but Lord, I do have enemies. There have been people who have set out against me and my family in different areas of life. I pray that You would have Your will in those situations. You chose to set David up as king and to conquer his enemies for Your own glory and purposes. Whether or not you choose to deliver me from opposition, I pray that my life honors and glorifies You as You work through me in your mercy.

Your Prayer:

Psalm 59:16-17 – But as for me, I shall sing of Your strength; Yes, I shall joyfully sing of Your lovingkindness in the morning, for You have been my stronghold and a refuge in the day of my distress. O my strength, I will sing praises to You; For God is my stronghold, the God who shows me lovingkindness.

My Prayer: Lord, I sing to You because of who You are. You are worthy of my praise. You are my safe place, my anchor in the storm, and a very merciful Father. Thank You for carrying me through this life. Thank You for Your lovingkindness.

Your Prayer:

Apply:

There are people in your life who are going to join the wicked in the Lake of Fire because they do not know Jesus as their personal savior.

1. Write down the names of one or two people you know that do not know Christ.
2. Pray for them to accept Him.
3. Pray for God to give you opportunities to share the gospel with them.
4. Now, watch for those opportunities and share the gospel!
5. When you have shared the gospel with this one or two, and they either accept or reject, start praying for another one or two.
6. Repeat forever.
7. If you are unsure about your own salvation, see the "How to Become a Christian" section at the end of this book.

Memorize:

Psalm 59:16a – But as for me, I shall sing of Your strength;

Journal Additional Prayers and Thoughts

Day 23 – Hope for the Faint Hearted

Read and Meditate:

Psalm 60:1 – Psalm 61:8

Learn:

You might not have a physical adversary who is constantly on the attack against you. However, if you are a child of God you do have a spiritual adversary. There is an enemy who wants to trap you, discourage you, and hinder the work of God in your life. He will provide excuses for you to disengage from your church family. He will lie to you about your value and worth. He will try to worm his way into every part of your life until he has robbed you of all joy.

You can try to fight against your adversary, but you will not get very far. You will quickly become weakened, exhausted, and ready to give up. There is only one way to fight against the devil and that is to PRAY! Only on your knees, calling on the power of God will you witness victory over the enemy. God is the one who fights for us when we call upon Him. Often, God will require you to act as He directs you toward victory. He always requires obedience from His children, even in the face of adversity.

When our enemy has worn us down, and we are too tired to go another step we must remember that God brings us rest. He is our refuge, and He desires to protect us and shelter us from the attacks of our enemy. It might not seem like it because He does not always remove our obstacles. Sometimes, He allows us to stay in the turmoil of the situation, but He will always calm us and give us strength when we ask Him in faith and obedience.

There is no escape on this earth from the troubles that come upon us. I know that sounds bleak and hopeless. When we recognize the power of God in our lives; when we come to Him in prayer and obedience we are not left without hope. Instead, we gain the strength necessary to continue living in obedience to God's call and will for our lives.

Do you recognize the attacks of your enemy? Listen to how the Psalmist talks to God about his adversaries and learn to pray with that kind of boldness about your own enemy. God is our hope and He will fight for us!

Pray:
Psalm 60:11-12 – O give us help against the adversary, for deliverance by man is in vain. Through God we shall do valiantly, and it is He who will tread down our adversaries.

My Prayer: God, You alone can deliver me from the adversary. The attacks seem to be endless, and all my attempts to escape fall short. So, Lord, I am still. I will wait for Your deliverance. Help us fight the good fight however You see fit and I pray for Your help to deliver us from the attacks of evil against us and against the ministry You have entrusted to us.

Your Prayer:

Psalm 61:1-2 – Hear my cry, O God; Give heed to my prayer. From the end of the earth I call to You when my heart is faint; Lead me to the rock that is higher than I.

My Prayer: Lord, I do not understand why we are suffering is so many ways. I do know that You are the God who hears. I know that You hear my cries for help. More often I feel like my heart is always faint. I always need You, Lord! You are the Rock. You are the high place where I will be safe. You are the only one who can answer my prayers.

Your Prayer:

Psalm 61:4 – Let me dwell in Your tent forever; Let me take refuge in the shelter of Your wings.

My Prayer: Spread Your comfort over me like a mother hen covers her babies. Thank You for the cross that gave me the gift of open communion with You. I know I will dwell with You forever, thanks to Your salvation. You are my refuge and my shelter from the storms of life on this earth. The storms will end one day and then I will dwell in complete safety with You forever! I am so grateful for Your grace.

Your Prayer:

Apply:

Is your heart growing weary from the onslaught of attack from your adversary?

1. Ask God for deliverance.
2. Write out the things you are being overwhelmed by and talk to the Lord about them.
3. Find a biblical counselor to help you navigate this part of your journey.

Memorize:

Psalm 61:2 – From the end of the earth I call to You when my heart is faint; Lead me to the rock that is higher than I.

Journal Additional Prayers and Thoughts

Day 24 – Unshakeable

Read and Meditate:

Psalm 62:1 – Psalm 63:11

Learn:

Many years ago, my husband and I were in Jamaica. As I was laying out at the pool, overlooking the beach, I felt the concrete ground beneath me start to shake. It did not even phase me that we had just experienced a small earthquake. I was in my happy place! I had the beauty of the ocean and the Caribbean skies. I had the comfort and joy of laying out by the pool, watching the ocean without the itchy sand, and I was in Jamaica with the love of my life. No earthquake was about to ruin that for me! The staff began to hustle around just in case a larger quake was to follow. I sat up, turned over, and kept on sunbathing.

In a lot of ways, this experience has helped me remember the truths found in today's passage. We experience many "earthquakes" in life. There are times when the ground seems to be shaking beneath us. Death, sickness, cancer, divorce, job loss, bankruptcy, or a wayward child are all situations that will shake us to the core. The ground is unstable. The potential is there for a greater quake. Even the ongoing struggles of life can make us feel a bit unstable. Most of us have been affected in some way by one or more of these situations. When I find the ground trembling below me, I can come to Psalm 62 and remember that God is my firm foundation. He is my refuge. He is my stronghold. Infinitely greater than my "happy place" in Jamaica, God is my stable place in life.

The word that came to my mind as I read the passage today was "unshakeable." This should be a goal of every believer; not that life will never shake us up, but that we will find our footing quickly in the stability that God offers to His children. This stability does not come upon us magically when we become a Christian. Rather, stability is built in our life as we seek after God; thirsty, longing for Him, and trusting Him in every situation. As you meditate on and pray through the Word today, remember that you have a safe place when the earthquakes of life threaten to shake you. If you know Christ, you can be unshakeable!

Pray:
Psalm 62:1-2 – My soul waits in silence for God only; From Him is my salvation. He only is my rock and my salvation, My stronghold; I shall not be greatly shaken.

My Prayer: O God, I wish I could pray this in honesty all the time. You are my stronghold and I do not have to be shaken. Lord, teach me to wait and to silence my soul. I want to be so enamored by Your salvation and so settled in You that nothing shakes me anymore. Thank You for taking me through rough waters. Thank You for always protecting me and providing for me. Thank You for being my rock through life.

Your Prayer:

Psalm 62:8 – Trust in Him at all times, O people; Pour out your heart before Him; God is a refuge for us.

My Prayer: At all times, Lord. At all times I trust You. Even when things are not going the way I think they should. In the dark times and the good times, I will trust Your good plan. Thank You for always listening to the deepest suffering of my heart. Thank You for letting me pour my heart out before You. You are my safe place and You know how messy my prayers can get. Thank You for not rejecting me, but for providing a refuge for me. I will never fully understand, but I am so grateful!

Your Prayer:

Psalm 63:1 – O God, You are my God; I shall seek You earnestly; My soul thirsts for You, my flesh yearns for You, in a dry and weary land where there is no water.

My Prayer: This, God! This is my heart! I need You more and more every single day. The more I seek You, the more my soul longs for You. This life leaves me spent. It truly is a dry land, with nothing available to bring hope and healing. Only You bring true nourishment for my life. I need You, I long for You, and I thank You that You are not far from me. Thank You for Your Word and thank You for listening to my prayers.

Your Prayer:

Apply:

1. Spend some time praying about the earthquakes that you are going through currently. Whether it is a mild tremor or off the Richter scale, talk to the Lord about it.

2. Twice in Psalm 62, the psalmist chooses to wait in silence as he trusts the Lord through the trial. How does that look in your life?

3. Make a choice to pour it out to God and seek Him in His Word so that your soul can wait on His deliverance.

Memorize:

Psalm 62:6 – He only is my rock and my salvation, my stronghold; I shall not be shaken.

Journal Additional Prayers and Thoughts

Day 25 – Sharp Tongues and Bitter Speech

Read and Meditate:

Psalm 64:1 – Psalm 65:13

Learn:

"Sticks and stones will break my bones, but words will never hurt me." We were taught to sing this as children as a defense mechanism against those who hurt our feelings with their words. It served the purpose if the words were innocent, childish banter. It served the purpose if the one singing it was so sensitive that even gentle words offended. This song falls very short, however, when the words become more sinister and the motives become intentionally diabolical. Words do hurt, and they cut deep to the soul of the one they are spoken against.

The imagery in Psalm 64 brings vivid memories to mind of times in my own life that I have been the receiver of a sharp-tongued outrage; And, God forgive me, of times I have been the one with bitter speech about another. We are all guilty of using our words to harm others, and for that we must repent. Hopefully, we are not guilty of the conniving, evil-motived hate speech that is being described in this passage.

There is not good news for the one who verbally attacks, abuses, slanders, and holds secret meetings of gossip against the children of God. He will stand up for His own. When one shoots arrows of hate speech, God is the one who will shoot back. This should give strong warning for those who use their tongue for evil, and it should incite great comfort for His children who are under attack.

Notice, there is no mention of the Psalmist attacking back with words of his own. If you have been hurt by the words and actions of others, know that you have a loving God who will fight that battle for you. There is no need to retaliate in like manner. Focus on the Lord, dig deeper in His Word, and pray for God to handle the situation and to give you wisdom in your next steps. He is your refuge when the arrows of sharpened tongues and bitter speech leave a gaping wound in your heart.

Pray:
Psalm 64:2-4 – Hide me from the secret counsel of evildoers, from the tumult of those who do iniquity, who have sharpened their tongue like a sword. They aimed bitter speech as their arrow, to shoot from concealment at the blameless;

My Prayer: God, people are so mean! Why do people have to say such mean things? I cannot comprehend why this happens, yet I am sure that I have also been guilty of this. Forgive me when my words have hurt others. Shield me, Lord. Shield my husband. Shield my children. Help us to overlook harsh or evil words that they would not take root in our hearts. Protect us from anger and bitterness.

Your Prayer:

Psalm 64:7-10 – But God will shoot at them with an arrow; suddenly they will be wounded. So they will make him stumble; Their own tongue is against them; All who see them will shake the head. Then all men will fear, and they will declare the work of God, and will consider what He has done. The righteous man will be glad in the Lord and will take refuge in Him; And all the upright in heart will glory.

My Prayer: You are the one who takes vengeance, Lord. You alone know the hearts of every person. I trust You, God, to have Your way with those who have slandered and verbally abused Your children. God, my prayer is that all men would fear You and declare Your works and consider Your ways. You desire reconciliation, so build that heart in me too. Give me the strength to forgive and to leave them in Your hands.

Your Prayer:

Psalm 65:4 – How blessed is the one whom You choose and bring near to You to dwell in Your courts. We will be satisfied with the goodness of Your house, Your holy temple.

My Prayer: Even amid evil, we can rest knowing that we are blessed by You. Thank You for reminding me that this is not my home and the back biters are not my people. My joy, my longing, my satisfaction comes from You alone.

Your Prayer:

Apply:

1. Pay attention to how you speak to and about others. Is your tongue sharp? Are your words bitter?

2. Confess it to the Lord and ask forgiveness of those you have hurt.

3. If you have been devastated by people like the ones described in Psalm 64, please hold on to the Lord and let Him be your refuge.

4. Pray for those people, asking God to have His will with them and to give you wisdom in how to proceed without retaliating.

Memorize:

Psalm 64:10 – The righteous man will be glad in the Lord and will take refuge in Him; And all the upright in heart will glory.

Journal Additional Prayers and Thoughts

Day 26 – How Excited are You?

Read and Meditate:

Psalm 66:1 – Psalm 67:7

Learn:

Have you ever met someone who is a die-hard sports fan? They buy t-shirts, hats, posters, home décor, license plate covers, and anything else they can find that promotes their favorite team. They go to the games if they are able, and they scream along with the crowds to cheer on their team. They yell when an unfair call is made by the refs. They jump out of their seat in excitement when something big is about to happen. They have parties, inviting friends and family into their home to watch the game on TV. They tell anyone who will listen all about the big game, and they will talk for years about that awesome play from that one player, that one time.

Do you have that kind of excitement about God? Do you tell anyone who will listen all about the awesome things He has done? Do you have people into your home so you can share your excitement about the Lord? Do you shout and jump out of your seat when you are worshipping

Almighty God with fellow believers? Do you recognize what God is doing in your life?

The Psalmist in today's passage understood how awesome God is, and he was not afraid to be vocal about it. Even when he was speaking about the trials and testing that God was using to refine him, he still rejoiced. The Psalmist honored his vows, sacrificed to the Lord, praised Him, and told others about Him. All this BEFORE the promised Messiah came. How much more should we be sharing now that Jesus has come, and salvation is readily available to all who would receive it? We have every reason to jump and shout for joy as believers.

We must come to the place in our lives when we get excited about God and what He is doing around us. We must learn to brag about our God. It is impossible to over-exaggerate when it comes to sharing about how amazing God is. He exceeds our wildest imagination! Everything we have and everything we are comes from God alone. The fact that we woke up breathing today is only because God allowed it. We should shout for joy about that! Praise the Lord!

Pray:

Psalm 66:5 – Come and see the works of God, Who is awesome in His deeds toward the sons of men.

My Prayer: God, You are incredibly awesome. You have done amazing works, both revealed in Your Word and in my own life. I will not stop proclaiming Your works, helping everyone see how wonderful You are. Forgive me when I do not proclaim You enough and help me learn to share You more and more!

Your Prayer:

Psalm 66:16 – Come and hear, all who fear God, and I will tell of what He has done for my soul.

My Prayer: Not only have You done amazing works physically, but You have worked miracles in my own heart. You calm my spirit when I am afraid. You clean my conscience when You forgive my sins. You give me peace when I am worried and overwhelmed. Truly, You alone can do these things. Give me Your words as I share how You work in my life.

Your Prayer:

Psalm 67:5-7 – Let the peoples praise You, O God; Let all the peoples praise You. The earth has yielded its produce; God, our God, blesses us. God blesses us, that all the ends of the earth may fear Him.

My Prayer: God, I do pray for Your blessings. I pray more that I would be keenly aware of every blessing, and that I would boldly proclaim Your power so that others can praise Your name! Thank You for all the many ways You bless me far beyond what I deserve.

Your Prayer:

Apply:

Do something to proclaim God today. Here are a few ideas to get you started.

1. Tell someone about an answer to prayer
2. Ask someone if you can pray for them
3. Choose an attribute of God and share a post about it on social media
4. Share a Bible verse with someone
5. Turn up the worship music in your car, roll the windows down, and sing along
6. Invite a friend over to share with them what God has been doing in your life.

Memorize:

Psalm 66:20 – Blessed be God, Who has not turned away my prayer nor His lovingkindness from me.

Journal Additional Prayers and Thoughts

Day 27 – A Heavy Load

Read and Meditate:

Psalm 68:1 – Psalm 69:36

Learn:

Paralyzed. Your circumstances are just too much to bear. The weight of your burdens make you feel as if you are drowning just below the surface; able to see the light skimming on the top of the water, yet unable to reach it. You cannot breathe, your body hurts, and your spirit is breaking. You can see all the things you should be doing, but you cannot seem to put one foot in front of the other. You are stuck. You are depressed. You are paralyzed. But you are not alone!

Contrary to the belief of some, the Bible does not minimize the reality of depression and anxiety. If you are human, you have experienced some level of depression at some point in your life. If you have not yet, you will. The Bible is full of truth that points us to hope and deliverance from depression. Today's passage is especially poignant about the hope we have through God.

Look through Psalm 69 again and notice the descriptions the Psalmist uses to describe his feelings.

Weary (v 3), parched (v 3), estranged (v 8). There is no foothold (v 2). Certainly, circumstances come along that cause us great pain and anxiety. Did you notice, though, that God wants to carry these burdens for us? We have a God who loves us in our sin, carries us in our struggles, and delivers us from our depression. While the world offers empty chatter, God offers authentic help. He can offer this help because He experienced a heavy load Himself. He bore the burden of the cross, suffering reproach and shame so that you and I would have hope – both now and forever.

If you are carrying a heavy load that has you feeling stuck or paralyzed, please seek out someone who can walk alongside you during this time. You might ask your pastor or pastor's wife, a mentor or teacher from your church, or a professional biblical counselor. Do not be ashamed of asking for help. God designed us for community and as believers we are to help carry one another's burdens. Seeking counsel does not make you weak or immature. On the contrary, it takes a great amount of courage and maturity to recognize when you need support and even greater strength to ask for help.

Pray:

Psalm 68:19 – Blessed be the Lord, who daily bears our burden, the God who is our salvation. Selah.

My Prayer: Lord, just knowing that You are bearing my burdens for me – Every. Single. Day. – gives me such hope and comfort. Not only do You bear my burdens, but You count it as a blessing to do so! You alone are my salvation from sin to eternal life, and You alone are my salvation from trouble to Your peace. Thank You for bearing my burdens. They are just too heavy for me to carry.

Your Prayer:

Psalm 69:2-3 – I have sunk in deep mire, and there is no foothold; I have come into deep waters, and a flood overflows me. I am weary with my crying; my throat is parched; My eyes fail while I wait for my God.

My Prayer: I keep trying to carry my burden alone. God, help me! I am overwhelmed. My worries and expectations paralyze me as I cry out to You, waiting for Your rescue.

Yet, I trust You. I know that You are working, even if I do not see it.

Your Prayer:

Psalm 69: 13-14 – But as for me, my prayer is to You, O Lord, at an acceptable time; O God, in the greatness of Your lovingkindness, answer me with Your saving truth. Deliver me from the mire and do not let me sink; May I be delivered from my foes and from the deep waters.

My Prayer: Lord, Your timing is always perfect. Teach me to rest while I wait. Do not let me sink in my fears and emotions. Deliver my soul from turmoil and give me peace while I pray to You. Comfort my soul as I continue to serve You, one day at a time. Show me my next step. Un-paralyze me by Your power!

Your Prayer:

Apply:

What burdens are you carrying that are causing you to sink?

1. Make a list of these burdens
2. Ask the Lord to carry them for you.
3. Use today's memory verse as a prayer whenever you feel like you cannot wait for deliverance anymore.
4. Remember that His timing is always perfect.

Memorize:

Psalm 69:13b – O Lord, at an acceptable time; O God, in the greatness of Your lovingkindness, answer me with Your saving truth.

Journal Additional Prayers and Thoughts

Day 28 – A Lifelong Purpose

Read and Meditate:

Psalm 70:1 – Psalm 71:24

Learn:

Notice in today's reading how much space is devoted to the ongoing nature of our relationship with the Lord. Multiple times, the Psalmist uses the word "continually" to describe an aspect of his connection with God. He also refers to his youth and old age in several verses throughout chapter 71. The idea of constant interaction, consistent prayer, and continual worship sums up well the theme we see throughout the Psalms.

Life is difficult. Trials often seem never-ending. How many times have we seen the writers of the Psalms crying out for deliverance and help from the Lord? Yet, they always come back to the truth that God will deliver in His own way and His own time. We are to call out to Him, and then worship Him as we proclaim His greatness to everyone around us. Continually.

From youth to old age, our purpose is to petition, praise, and proclaim our Heavenly Father. We petition him when we call on Him for help. He is our deliverer. He is our refuge. He is our strength. We must never cease from praying to the Lord.

We praise Him in every circumstance. When He delivers us, we praise Him. When we are blessed, we praise Him. When we are depressed, we praise Him. We praise Him because He is worthy and deserving, not because He answers our prayers how we want or when we want. Praise Him when everything in life is going well and praise Him when everything in life seems to be falling apart. We praise Him always.

We then take every opportunity to proclaim Him. Tell of His greatness and power. Share about His answers to our prayers. We open our mouth and tell someone about the gospel of Jesus Christ. This is our purpose. This is how we join the Psalmist in saying, "My mouth is filled with Your praise and with Your glory all day long" (Ps 71:8). Ask the Lord to renew this purpose in your heart today as you pray through today's passage.

Pray:
Psalm 70:5 – But I am afflicted and needy; hasten to me, O God! You are my help and my deliverer; O Lord, do not delay.

My Prayer: God, thank You for the Psalms. Thank You for letting me know that I am not alone. Sometimes, I feel very repetitive in my prayers. It seems the troubles only multiply and my needs only grow. Yet, here You show me how much You delight in coming to my rescue. So, I pray again – deliver me, Lord. Come to my rescue in my time of need. You alone can help me and deliver me.

Your Prayer:

Psalm 71:5-6 – For You are my hope; O Lord God, You are my confidence from my youth. By You I have been sustained from my birth; You are He who took me from my mother's womb; My praise is continually of You.

My Prayer: I am forever grateful that You got a hold of my heart as a little girl. I praise You for sustaining me, protecting me, and loving me so tangibly. Even from my birth, You were orchestrating the events of my life, and I praise You for the life I have lived. Thank You for Your many blessings.

Your Prayer:

Psalm 71:17-18 – O God, You have taught me from my youth, and I still declare Your wonderous deeds. And even when I am old and gray, O God, do not forsake me, until I declare Your strength to this generation, Your power to all who are to come.

My Prayer: Lord, in this stage of my life, I hold on to this verse so tightly! Thank You for teaching me and guiding me these first 40 years. As I begin a new phase of life, I pray for Your strength and Your power to point me in all the right directions. Thank You for never forgetting me. Thank You for using me for Your service in every stage of my life. I pray for clear direction as I continue to serve You.

Your Prayer:

Apply:

1. Whatever stage of life you are in, identify three areas where you can proclaim the greatness of God.

2. Even as you call on Him for help, recognize that He has a purpose for what you are going through and where you are in life.

3. Use your purpose and circumstances for His glory today and the rest of your life!

Memorize:

Psalm 71:1 – In You, O Lord, I have taken refuge; Let me never be ashamed.

Journal Additional Prayers and Thoughts

Day 29 – God is All You Need

Read and Meditate:

Psalm 72:1 – Psalm 73:28

Learn:

Have you ever met a child who wants everything they see on tv, at the store, or pretty much anywhere in life? I was that child. Somebody must have really impressed on me that there is a big difference between something I want and something I need. I took that information and translated it that I no longer *wanted* anything. Instead, I *needed* everything! I *needed* that baby doll. I *needed* that beautiful dress. I *needed* those shoes.

Unfortunately, my hunger to satisfy my "need" followed me into adulthood. I *need* a better job, I *need* more money, I *need* a new car, I *need* people to love me on my terms. It took a few years of living in the real world and growing in my walk with the Lord to recognize that nothing is a true need except life with my Heavenly Father. He knows our actual needs, and He will provide for those needs in His own way and in His own time.

Comparison feeds these false needs. Whether you are in poverty, middle class, or the high elite, you can always find someone who has more than you have. There will always be the temptation to look on with envy at the life of another. When we do, we open our hearts up to jealousy, envy, and discontentment. These forms of covetousness are sin and must be rooted out of the life of the believer.

Psalm 73 walks us through the process of this sin of envy, and the bitterness that it can create in our hearts. It begins with a vivid description of how the Psalmist views the prosperous man. They have plenty to eat, they are healthy, and they do not have any troubles. Then, he recognizes how close he comes to stumbling because of his envy. He then realizes how he must look to God when bitterness is ruling his life. The Psalmist wisely ends with the proper awareness that "the nearness of God is my good." Nothing else matters in comparison to the presence of Almighty God.

What is most important in your life? Is it all the belongings, status, and wealth that you think you need? Are you more concerned about having a fulfilling career than you are having a fulfilling relationship with Christ? I hope that we can all grasp the reality that God is all we need! Without Him, nothing else matters.

Pray:

Psalm 72:18-19 – Blessed be the Lord God, the God of Israel, who alone works wonders. And blessed be His glorious name forever; And may the whole earth be filled with His glory. Amen, and Amen.

My Prayer: God, You have worked so many amazing wonders in my life! You are blessed. You are amazing. You are glorious. I will praise Your name and exalt Your glory in my world. It is only You that holds this world together. You alone are worthy of my honor and my praise.

Your Prayer:

Psalm 73:2-3 – But as for me, my feet came close to stumbling, my steps had almost slipped. For I was envious of the arrogant as I saw the prosperity of the wicked.

My Prayer: While You are awesome and glorious, Lord, I am weak and sinful. It is so discouraging to me when I see unsaved who are living in luxury and then I see Your servants struggling to put food on the table. I admit, I have sinned and given in to envy. Lord, forgive me! Heal my heart of jealousy and bitterness. Keep my foot from stumbling over my own sin!

Your Prayer:

Psalm 73:26 – My flesh and my heart my fail, but God is the strength of my heart and my portion forever.

My Prayer: Thank You, God, for being my strength. I fail in my humanity and You are always faithful to pick me back up and draw me to Yourself. I am weak, O Lord, and need You desperately. You are my strength. You hold my heart close to You, and You alone are all I ever need!

Your Prayer:

Apply:

Search deep in your heart. What are some of the things that you think you need? What are you looking to for satisfaction in life other than the Lord?

1. Make a list and then cross off one thing from that list that you are no longer going to desire or envy.
2. Write next to the item you crossed off, "All I need is Jesus."
3. Pray for release from that item.
4. Seek out ways to actively prove that you no longer need that item.
5. Challenge yourself to work this way through the entire list over time, asking God for freedom from envy and the desire for false needs.

Memorize:

Psalm 72:18 – Blessed be the Lord God, the God of Israel, who alone works wonders.

Journal Additional Prayers and Thoughts

Day 30 – A Response to Persecution

Read and Meditate:

Psalm 74:1 – Psalm 75:10

Learn:

God's people are not strangers to persecution and suffering. Sometimes, God chooses to deliver His children, and other times God uses the persecution to fulfill a greater purpose. The psalmist in today's passage is crying out to the Lord about the suffering of His people and the destruction of the house of the Lord. While we would like to think that this type of suffering only happened in Bible times, the reality is that Christians continue to suffer at the hands of evil to this day.

Maybe you have never experienced physical persecution or witnessed the destruction of your church, but you may have heard about the suffering of others in the world. Either way, there are great truths here that we must remember as we think about persecution today.

Truth #1 – The world is against Christ, and they prove it by setting up their own standard for life. The symbols that the world uses and elevates are in direct contradiction to the Lord. Therefore, persecution is very real and closer to home than you might think.

Truth #2 – God can put an end to persecution at any time He wants to. The Psalmist points all attention to God as he both reveals how able He is as well as His authority to do what He wants to do.

Truth #3 – God will judge in His own time, and we must trust Him. One day, all evil will be judged once and for all. Until that day, we must trust and obey the Lord at any cost.

Truth #4 – We can, and we must praise the Lord with thanksgiving, even when suffering persecution. God is worthy to be praised in every situation; both the good and the bad. We should call out to the Lord to deliver, but we must trust Him whether deliverance comes or not. The ultimate purpose is that we would share the Lord with others, tell them of His mighty works, and pray for the salvation of their souls.

Pray:

Psalm 74:7-8 – They have burned Your sanctuary to the ground; They have defiled the dwelling place of Your name. They said in their heart, "Let us completely subdue them." They have burned all the meeting places of God in the land.

My Prayer: Lord God, my heart is so heavy. The persecution of Your church is ever present around our world. The evil behind this persecution is heart wrenching. I know that You could stop the persecution, and I pray that You do. More than that, I pray that people will come to know You through the blood of Jesus as they witness the steadfastness of Your persecuted saints. I pray that through persecution, we would draw ever closer to You.

Your Prayer:

Psalm 74:22-23 – Arise, O God, and plead Your own cause; Remember how the foolish man reproaches You all day long. Do not forget the voice of Your adversaries, the uproar of those who rise against You which ascends continually.

My Prayer: Lord, I know You see, and I know that You do not forget. Please stand up for these Christians who are losing their lives. If it is Your will, put a hedge of protection around Your people. If persecution is in the plan,

I pray that we would stand strong against it. Either way, we need You doing the work for us. Please stand in our gap, O God.

Your Prayer:

Psalm 75:1-3 – We give thanks to You, O God, we give thanks, for Your name is near; Men declare Your wondrous works. "When I select an appointed time, it is I who judge with equity. The earth and all who dwell in it melt; It is I who have firmly set its pillars." Selah.

My Prayer: You are just. You are fair. You are good, all the time. I will praise You when life is peaceful, and I will praise You when evil abounds all around us and life gets tough. You will judge evil at Your appointed time. You are God, and I am not. It is not for me to know Your timing; it is for me to simply trust. Thank You for being God and thank You for always being near.

Your Prayer:

Apply:

1. Pray for missionaries who are suffering persecution for the gospel of Christ.

2. Do an internet search for "Christian persecution" and read articles about areas of the world where persecution is common.

3. Ask your pastor for information on missionaries who are in persecuted areas of the world.

4. Read stories and see how you can pray for thousands of missionaries all over the world. A good place to start is visiting wmu.com, namb.net, or imb.org

5. Think about ways that you can support these missionaries through prayer, mission trips, financial gifts, or other endeavors.

Memorize:

Psalm 75:9 – But as for me, I will declare it forever; I will sing praises to the God of Jacob.

Journal Additional Prayers and Thoughts

How to Become a Christian

1. **Recognize** that you are a sinner and agree with God that you cannot be good enough to earn your way into Heaven. The judgement against sin is separation from God and an eternity in the Lake of Fire.

"For all have sinned and fall short of the glory of God."
Romans 3:23

"As it is written, 'There is none righteous, not even one; there is none who understands, there is none who seeks for God; all have turned aside, together they have become useless; there is none who does good, there is not even one.'" Romans 3:10-12

"For all of us have become like one who is unclean, and all our righteous deeds are like a filthy garment; and all of us wither like a leaf, and our iniquities, like the wind, take us away." Isaiah 64:6

"For the wages of sin is death, but the free gift of God is eternal life in Christ Jesus our Lord." Romans 6:23

"And if anyone's name was not found written in the book of life, he was thrown into the lake of fire." Revelation 20:15

2. **Repent** of your sins. Turn from the direction you are headed, confessing your sins to God.

"Therefore repent and return, so that your sins may be wiped away, in order that times of refreshing may come from the presence of the Lord." Acts 3:19

"For thus the Lord God, the Holy One of Israel, has said, 'In repentance and rest you will be saved..'" Isaiah 30:15a

"Got has granted to the Gentiles also the repentance that leads to life." Acts 11:18b

3. **Receive** God's free gift of salvation. He offers eternal life to all who believe. Simply ask Him to save you from your sin today!

"For God so loved the world, that He gave His only begotten Son, that whoever believes in Him shall not perish, but have eternal life." John 3:16

"That if you confess with your mouth Jesus as Lord, and believe in your heart that God raised Him from the dead, you will be saved; for with the heart a person believes, resulting in righteousness, and with the mouth he confesses, resulting in salvation." Romans 10:9-10

"They said, 'Believe in the Lord Jesus, and you will be saved,'" Acts 16:31a

"For by grace you have been saved through faith; and that not of yourselves, it is the gift of God; not as a result of works, so that no one may boast." Ephesians 2:8-9

Methods of Scripture Memory

1. Word removal method

This method is easiest done on a white board, chalk board, or computer document. You will write out the verse you are memorizing. Read the verse a few times out loud. Now, erase one word. Read the entire verse a few more times out loud. Erase another word. Do this until you have a blank screen in front of you!

2. Repetition method

Write out the verse on a 3x5 card and place it somewhere that you will see it multiple times a day or carry it with you all day long. Read the verse every chance you get and repeat whatever you can remember from memory throughout the day.

3. Block section method

This is especially helpful for larger verses. You can do it right in your Bible or you can write the verse out and do it on paper. Simply draw a short line at every natural break in the verse. Memorize one small section at a time until you have the whole thing memorized. Here is what it will look like:

For God so loved the world, | that He gave His only begotten Son, | that whoever believes in Him | shall not perish, | but have eternal life. | John 3:16

4. First letter method

This is my favorite method if you are memorizing a lot of verses and you want to continue to review them over time. Use one of the other methods to become as familiar as you can with the verse. Then, write out the first letter of each word in a notebook. Using only the first letters, review your memory verse. Keep a notebook of all the verses you have memorized and review them often. Here is what it will look like:

For all have sinned and fall short of the glory of God. Romans 3:23

Write in notebook: F A H S A F S O T G O G. R 3:23

About the Author

Melissa Goepfrich is a Christian author, speaker, and women's ministry leader. She and her husband spent their first 15 years together serving in youth ministry in their hometown of South Bend, IN. During that time, Melissa began to follow a call on her life to leave youth ministry and begin serving and teaching the women in the church. In 2014, her husband answered a call to become a senior pastor, and they packed up their three children and moved to Warsaw, IN to revitalize Warsaw Baptist Church.

Melissa was saved when she was just five years old. Through the ministry of many faithful servants of Christ, Melissa was introduced to Jesus and grew in her walk with Him. God's Word became very dear to her early on as she learned to memorize, read and study every detail. Her passion has always been to reach out to those who are hurting, show them the love of God, and teach them how to find hope and healing. This only happens through a relationship with Jesus Christ and living in obedience and submission to His Word.

You can connect with Melissa on Instagram or Facebook @melissagoepfrichauthor or on her website www.melissagoepfrich.org

Made in the USA
Lexington, KY
24 October 2019